Healthy Food
for
Babies
and
Toddlers

Expert advice from
Dr Helen Crawley, Registered Public Health Nutritionist

Cover design by
Mary Cartwright and Laura Hammonds

Additional illustrations by
Ruth Russell

Food photography by
Howard Allman

Food preparation and styling by
Dagmar Vesely

Healthy Food
for
Babies
and Toddlers

Henny Fordham

Illustrated by Shelagh McNicholas

Designed by Laura Hammonds
and Joanne Kirkby

Edited by Felicity Brooks

Internet links

For further information about Usborne Parents' Guides
and to visit the websites recommended in this book, go to
www.usborne-quicklinks.com
Click on 'Parents' Guides' or type in the keywords 'healthy food for babies'.

Contents

Toddler meals (1 – 3 years)

Fun with food

Special diets and activity

Useful information

A healthy diet

This section looks at what babies and toddlers need in terms of nutrition and what makes up a healthy diet. It outlines some concerns about food production and processing, and the advantages of making your own meals. There is also advice on buying baby food, reading labels and on food requirements for different ages and stages.

At a glance

Why a healthy diet in childhood is so important

An overview of what babies and toddlers
need at different ages and stages

How babies' and toddlers' dietary needs are
different from those of older children and adults

Choosing and cooking food for your baby,
buying baby food and reading labels

Hygiene and safety when preparing food
and feeding little children

A good start

The food that you give your baby or toddler provides them with the energy and the nutrients that they need to grow, develop and fight illness. The more nutritious and balanced their diet is, the better their bodies – and brains – will work. Children's diets also have a major impact on their long-term health, so what you feed your baby or toddler really is of vital importance.

This book offers lots of information, ideas, suggestions, tips and tactics for how to get babies and toddlers to eat well, without your having to spend hours preparing meals or buy lots of complicated ingredients. It brings together the latest advice about nutrition and children's diets and includes ideas and recipes for simple, healthy meals, snacks and drinks suitable for different ages. There's also plenty about how to get children to like good food from an early age and how to deal with, or prevent, 'fussy' eating.

Eating habits, good or bad, develop early.

Did you know?

Fat is vital for nerve formation in early childhood. Find out about 'good' and 'bad' fats for babies and toddlers on page 11.

Omega-3 fatty acids found in oil-rich fish are thought by some scientists to play a key role in children's brain development. Find out more about fish on page 58.

Babies under a year old should have less than 1g of salt a day as their kidneys cannot cope with it. Find out what else you should avoid giving them on page 29.

High-fibre foods such as bran cereals, wholemeal pasta and brown rice are not suitable for little children. Find out more on page 10.

A recent study found that children whose diet includes plenty of fruit, vegetables and fish are less likely to develop asthma and allergies. Find out more about allergies on pages 78 to 79.

The impact of a healthy diet begins even before a baby is born, so if you eat well during pregnancy, and while breast-feeding, this is the first step in ensuring a good start for your baby. When they are ready to start on solids, at about six months, you can begin to introduce a wide and varied range of foods and help your baby develop good eating patterns, which can last a lifetime.

Ages and stages

Here is some general information about what babies and toddlers should eat and drink up to the age of three. These stages correspond to the sections of the book where you can find a lot more detail and ideas for meals and snacks.

Birth to six months

For the first six months babies can get all the nutrients and fluid they need from breast or formula milk. Newborns need to feed frequently as they have tiny stomachs, but most settle into a pattern of feeds from about six weeks. It's best to follow what your baby tells you and let them feed when they want, for as long as they want. They show they've had enough by falling asleep or letting go of the breast or bottle.

Six to eight months

Most babies are ready to start on foods alongside milk from about six months and it's important to start weaning about this time. The idea is to introduce your baby to new tastes and textures so that they will be able to get enough nutrients from a varied diet when they start to reduce their intake of breast or formula milk and when they move on to cow's milk. Between six and eight months babies should also get used to lumpy textures and start to hold foods and feed themselves.

Weaning may start with a tiny spoonful of purée, but by nine months babies can be eating all kinds of mashed foods.

Did you know?

Most babies have growth spurts at around ten days, six weeks and three months. At these times they may want to feed more often and for longer.

Find out about equipment for bottle-feeding on page 20.

Safety points

If your baby was premature, talk to your doctor or health visitor before starting weaning at six months as your baby may not be ready for solids.

If you choose to wean your baby before six months, talk to your health visitor or doctor as there are certain foods that should be avoided.

Nine to eleven months

By nine months your baby should be eating three meals a day as well as some healthy snacks in between. Babies will start to reduce their milk intake as they get more energy from food. At this stage they can eat chopped and minced foods and foods mashed with a fork, along with a variety of finger foods. Many babies will have their first teeth now and need to learn how to chew. It's also a good idea to involve your baby in family meals as much as possible, offering them a wide range of some of the same foods that you eat.

Food from a year old

From a year old, your baby can join in with family meals (if you follow a few guidelines) and start drinking full-fat cow's milk as their main drink instead of breast milk or formula milk (though there is no reason to stop breast-feeding if you both want to continue). Many children are now starting to stand up or are taking their first steps and, as they become more active, they need a varied and energy-rich diet for their growth and development. Children under two still have very small stomachs so need small meals with healthy snacks in between.

Useful tip

You can download a printable feeding chart from the Usborne Quicklinks Website (see page 91).

How much food does a toddler need?

• Children's appetites vary greatly so be guided by your own toddler as to how big a portion should be.

• Don't force your child to finish food when they don't want to.

• Don't refuse to give more food if your child is still hungry.

• If your toddler is eating a range of foods and making good progress, try not to worry about how much (or how little) they eat.

Make sure your toddler eats a variety of foods from each of these groups:

Fruit and vegetables

Full-fat milk, yogurt and cheese

Bread, cereal, rice, pasta, potatoes, maize

Lean meat, fish, eggs and pulses (or vegetarian alternatives)

Give toddlers only very limited amounts of sugary, fatty foods such as cakes and cookies.

Nutrition for babies and toddlers

Babies' and toddlers' nutritional needs are much greater than those of adults as they are growing and developing so fast. Babies grow more in their first year than at any time during the rest of their life, so their foods need to be rich in energy, protein, vitamins and minerals. Up until six months, babies can get all the nutrients they need from breast milk (or formula milk) and this should continue to provide a lot of what they need for the first year, with solid food gradually replacing it as the main source of nutrition.

By the time babies are a year old, their diet needs to contain all the main food groups (see left) to provide protein, fat, carbohydrates, vitamins and minerals. Eating a variety of foods is the most reliable way for a child to take in what they need to stay healthy.

Babies and toddlers need foods rich in energy and nutrients for growth and development.

Useful tip

You can find out more about important vitamins and minerals and which foods are their main sources on pages 86 and 87.

A varied diet

A toddler's diet needs to include foods from each of these groups each day:

• Full-fat milk and dairy products such as cheese and yogurt for protein, calcium, vitamins and fat

• Lean meat, fish, eggs, pulses and lentils for protein, vitamins and minerals including iron

• Bread and other starchy foods such as rice, pasta, potatoes, yams, breakfast cereals and oats for energy, vitamins, minerals and fibre

• At least five child-size portions of fruit and vegetables for vitamins, minerals and fibre

Fibre in the diet

Babies and toddlers should generally have a diet that provides lots of calories and nutrients in a small amount of food. Although adults are advised to eat a high-fibre diet, the opposite is recommended for children under five. They find high-fibre foods such as some bran cereals, brown rice and wholewheat pasta very filling, and so do not eat enough food to get all the nutrients they need. Instead, young children should get their fibre from fruit and vegetables, beans and other pulses, and other cereal foods.

Fat facts

Babies and toddlers need fat for energy and growth and to help their bodies absorb essential vitamins, and in their first year babies should get about half their total energy from fat. Fats can be saturated (from foods such as meat and dairy products) or unsaturated (from plant oils, oily fish, nuts, seeds and avocados). While adults should cut down on saturated fats, it is important that babies and toddlers have full-fat milk and dairy produce up to the age of two. They also need unsaturated fats to provide essential fatty acids which their bodies can't manufacture and which are vital for their brain development.

Oily fish, plant oils, nuts, seeds, olives and avocados are all good sources of unsaturated fat.

Carbohydrates

'Starchy' carbohydrates in foods such as bread, rice, pasta and potatoes provide glucose, which is the most important source of energy for muscles and other tissues and organs, including the brain. Once babies are weaned, they need a regular intake of such starchy foods.

Sugars are a form of carbohydrate found in milk, fruit and vegetables. When they are part of the structure of a food they don't damage teeth, but once extracted from plants (such as sugar beet and cane, or fruit) and added to other foods, they can damage them. Sugar-added foods should be eaten only in small amounts and at mealtimes.

Fats to avoid

• Avoid foods which have 'hydrogenated', 'partially hydrogenated', or 'trans-fat' on the label. These saturated fats are not needed in anyone's diet.

• Use vegetable oils such as olive, rapeseed or soya bean oil for cooking, rather than butter or lard.

• Choose lean meat and trim visible fat from meat before you cook it.

Protein

Protein is also needed for growth, so babies and toddlers need a bigger proportion of it in their diet than adults do. Protein should not, however, be the major part of a baby's meal as a high-protein diet could put a strain on their kidneys. Breast or formula milk provides all the protein babies need up to six months, but during weaning you should soon introduce small quantities of protein-rich foods such as lean meat, eggs, cheese, fish, pulses and ground nuts.

Whole nuts and seeds must not be given to under-fives in case they choke on them, but ground nuts and seeds are good sources of protein.

Choosing and cooking food

Cooking your baby's food yourself, rather than relying on ready-made baby meals, allows you to keep control over what they eat and helps ensure they get the nutrients they need. There are some other good reasons to cook listed on the left. Any food is only ever as good as the ingredients that go into it, and many people are concerned about the quality, safety and nutritional content of the food they buy. Some of the main concerns are outlined here.

GM foods

Genetically modified (GM) foods are made from genetically modified plants and animals which have had their DNA altered through genetic engineering to give them new properties, such as resistance to herbicides. There's no evidence so far to show that GM food is unsafe, and in many countries GM crops are widely grown. However, the long-term impact of growing and eating GM foods is not known. Those who oppose genetic engineering say there is no way to ensure GM plants and animals remain under control, and that the use of this technology carries potential risks to farmed and wild ecosystems.

Cooking for your baby...

• Means you can provide the freshest and most nutritious meals possible, as you stay in control of the ingredients.

• Lets babies get used to the taste of 'real' food from an early age.

• Makes it easier to feed your baby the same food as the rest of the family.

• Works out cheaper — jars of baby food are very expensive for the quantity of food you are buying.

Did you know?

In the European Union, Japan, Malaysia and Australia, if a product contains GM ingredients it has to be labelled. Foods that are sold as 'organic' cannot contain GM ingredients.

Good butchers can tell you where meat comes from.

Pesticide residues

Non-organic crops can be regularly treated with chemical pesticides to kill unwanted pests, weeds and diseases and small amounts can remain in the crop after it is harvested. This is known as the residue. Under European law, there are strict limits on the levels of pesticide residues allowed in food, including formula milk and manufactured baby foods, but the long-term effect of consuming pesticide residues is not known.

Most organic food is produced without using pesticides because organic methods avoid using them. There are strict standards on what farmers are allowed to do when producing food that will be sold as 'organic'. Farmers are allowed to use a very limited range of pesticides on organic crops, but only as a last resort and only on some crops.

About additives

Food additives are substances that are added to food during processing to preserve or enhance its flavour or to improve its taste and appearance. There are thousands in use today of both natural and artificial origin, including colours, preservatives, antioxidants, sweeteners, flavour enhancers, emulsifiers, thickeners and gelling agents. European Union legislation requires most additives used in foods to be labelled clearly in the list of ingredients, either by name or by an E number. This allows you to avoid foods containing specific additives if you wish.

A recent scientific study has shown evidence of a link between certain food colourings and preservatives and changes in some young children's mood and behaviour. These additives are used in a number of foods, including soft drinks, sweets, cakes and ice cream. They have not been banned, but are listed by name and E number on the right if you want to avoid them.

Pesticide residues may be present in:

• Fresh, frozen or canned fruit and vegetables.

• Processed food and drink made from a crop treated with pesticides (e.g. fruit juice or bread).

• Fresh or processed animal products, if the animals have been fed on crops treated with pesticides.

Washing or peeling non-organic vegetables can remove some pesticide residues.

Additives to avoid
• Sunset yellow (E110)
• Quinoline yellow (E104)
• Carmoisine (E122)
• Allura red AC (E129)
• Tartrazine (E102)
• Ponceau 4R (E124)
• Sodium benzoate (E211)

Organic food

Because organic farming is less intensive than conventional farming, foods produced by this method often cost more. However, many people believe organic foods are healthier and taste better, and there is some evidence that they may contain higher amounts of some nutrients, such as antioxidants and some minerals. It's important to make sure that children's diets are varied and contain lots of fruit and vegetables, whether these are organic or not.

Buying baby food

It can be useful to have a few jars, cans and packets of baby food in the cupboard, but don't let them replace home-made foods altogether. If you buy baby foods, check labels so you can be aware of what your baby is eating. No artificial colours or preservatives or GM ingredients are allowed into baby food by law (in Europe) but recent research found that many cereals and biscuits contained added sugar, and more than 12 per cent of non-organic baby foods were contaminated with pesticide residues. Many baby foods have water as the main ingredient, whether they are organic or not, and some may have smaller amounts of the main ingredients than you'd include in a similar home-made version.

Check 'use by' and 'best before' dates, and that the seals on cans or jars of baby food are intact.

What is organic food?

• Organic food is grown without (or with the minimum use of) artificial pesticides and fertilizers.

• Organic meat comes from animals reared without the routine use of antibiotics, growth regulators or intensive livestock systems ('factory farming').

• Organic food production must be approved by a certified organization such as the Soil Association (whose logo is shown on packaging).

• Organic food cannot be genetically modified, or irradiated (a process that exposes food to electron beams, X-rays or gamma rays).

• Organic baby food cannot have iron added to it as this cannot be organically sourced.

What is 'free-range'?

• The term 'free-range' can be applied to eggs, meat and dairy products.

• In Europe it means farmers have adhered to certain standards of animal welfare.

• During the day the animals have access to the outdoors to graze or forage.

Reading labels

Food labels provide a lot of information, but the terms can be confusing. There are rules that all food manufacturers must follow to protect consumers from false claims or misleading descriptions, and clear guidelines on what labels on baby foods can and can't show. You can find out more on the Usborne Quicklinks Website (see page 91).

(see page 91)

Useful tip
A product called 'Organic Beef Casserole' will contain a higher proportion of organic ingredients than one which says 'Contains organic carrots' (for example).

This label is from a can of baby 'pasta bolognese'.

If any of the following foods, which may cause allergic reactions, are used they must be printed on the label:

- *celery*
- *cereals containing gluten (wheat, barley, rye and oats)*
- *crustaceans (such as lobster and crab)*
- *eggs*
- *fish*
- *milk*
- *mustard*
- *nuts (such as almonds, hazelnuts, walnuts, Brazil nuts, cashews, pecans)*
- *peanuts*
- *sesame seeds*
- *soya beans*
- *sulphur dioxide and sulphites (preservative)*

The amount of vitamins and minerals are given as a percentage of the Recommended Daily Amount (RDA), which has been determined by nutritionists.

No artificial colours or preservatives or GM ingredients are allowed into baby food by law (in Europe) so these are not exceptional qualities.

INGREDIENTS

Tomatoes (31%), Water, Pasta (21%) (made from Wheat), Beef (10%), Carrots, Cornflour, Herb Extracts, Yeast Extract, Natural Flavourings, Vegetable Oil, Iron Sulphate

CONTAINS

Gluten, Wheat

NUTRITION	(PER 100g)
Energy	274kJ/65kcal
Protein	3.3g
Carbohydrate	9.2g
(of which sugars)	(2.2g)
Fat	1.6g
(of which saturates)	(0.7g)
Fibre	0.5g
Sodium	Trace
Iron	1.0mg*

*17% of RDA

No added preservatives
No artificial colours
No GM ingredients
No added salt

Ingredients must be listed in order of weight, so if water is first, the product contains a high proportion of water. This also lets you look for ingredients you may want to avoid.

Manufacturers don't have to provide nutrition information (unless they are making a claim such as that a product is low in fat) but when they do, the information given must always be given as values per 100g or per 100ml of food. This is what it must contain:

The energy value of the food shown in kilojoules (kJ) and kilocalories (kcal).

The amount of protein, carbohydrate and fat shown in grams (g)

If the food claims to be high in fibre or low in fat, salt or sugar it must include the amounts of sugars, saturates, fibre and sodium in grams (g).

Some labels now include details about other nutrients such as vitamin and mineral content and quantities of fatty acids or cholesterol.

Do nappy-changing away from food preparation areas and wash your hands afterwards.

• Keep the kitchen extra clean – especially the floor when babies start to crawl.

• Wipe plastic bibs, highchair trays and table-tops before and after every meal.

• Wash or replace dishcloths and wiping cloths regularly.

• Teach young children about hand-washing as soon as they are ready.

• Keep dirty nappies away from food, and food preparation areas.

• Wash your hands after changing and handling dirty nappies.

Hygiene and health

Good kitchen hygiene and good personal hygiene are especially important when feeding babies and toddlers, to help control the spread of harmful germs. Young children's immune systems are not fully developed until they are two years old, and up until this age they are especially susceptible to stomach bugs, including gastroenteritis. Good hygiene can prevent such infections being passed on.

Make sure you always wash your hands in warm, soapy water before making food for your baby, and that any bottles and utensils you use to make up milk feeds have been sterilized (using one of the methods described on page 20). Breast milk is naturally sterile, but you should still wash your hands before each feed as you may need to put a finger in your baby's mouth to break the suction. When you start the process of weaning your baby, it will not be necessary to sterilize your baby's food-making equipment, but if you use bottles these still need to be sterilized, and everything you use for food preparation must be scrupulously clean. There are some good general hygiene rules to follow on the left.

Good hygiene can help little babies to stay happy and healthy.

0 — 6 months

Milk is the first food for all babies. Whether this is breast milk, formula milk or, later on, cow's or soya milk, milk contains the essential nutrients for the healthy development of a child. The World Health Organisation recommends that babies are fed exclusively on breast milk (or formula milk) for the first six months of their lives and that it should continue to be a significant part of their diet into their second year.

At a glance

Why breast-feeding is good for you and your baby

What to eat and what not to eat when breast-feeding

Equipment you need for bottle-feeding

How to prepare bottle feeds safely, including methods of sterilizing equipment

Getting ready for weaning your baby, including equipment you will need

Breast-feeding

Breast-feeding is the most natural way to feed a baby, but it doesn't always come easily to first-time mothers and it may take some practice and perseverance to get established. However, there is no doubt that breast milk gives babies the best start in life and that they benefit from its unique properties for the whole period they are breast-fed.

What is breast milk?

Breast milk is made by a woman's body specifically for her baby and contains all the energy, protein, fat, carbohydrates, vitamins and minerals the baby needs for the first six months of life in an easily digestible form. It also contains antibodies and anti-infective agents which help protect the baby from illness. In the first few days following birth, a new mother's breasts produce colostrum, a creamy, yellowish milk which is particularly rich in protein and anti-infective agents and which helps build up the baby's own immune system. After a few days this is replaced by breast milk. Breast milk changes during a feed: the 'foremilk' at the beginning quenches a baby's thirst; the 'hindmilk' is higher in fat to satisfy the baby's hunger.

Useful tip

For links to sources of support and advice about breast-feeding, visit the Usborne Quicklinks Website (see page 91).

What to eat

When you are breast-feeding, it's especially important to eat a varied and balanced diet:

• At least five portions of fruit and vegetables a day

• Lots of starchy carbohydrates such as pasta, rice, bread and potatoes for energy

• Foods rich in fibre such as beans, lentils, wholegrain bread and breakfast cereals

• Protein from lean meat, chicken, eggs and pulses, and fish at least twice a week

• Dairy foods such as milk, cheese and yogurt

• At least 1.2 litres (2 pints) of fluid a day (milk, fruit juice and water are good choices)

• A daily 10 microgram (mcg) supplement of vitamin D

It's important not to become dehydrated when you are breast-feeding, so have a drink to hand.

Why is it so good for babies?

Breast milk provides everything that young babies need for growth, optimum brain development and a healthy immune system up to the age of six months. Breast-fed babies are more able to fight off infection, are less likely to suffer from chest and ear infections, stomachaches and constipation, and they may also be less likely to develop eczema and asthma than bottle-fed babies.

Breast milk is always available and at the right temperature, and as there is no chance of the milk becoming contaminated, breast-fed babies are less likely to get stomach upsets or gastroenteritis. When a baby is upset or ill, feeding provides comfort and aids their recovery. Breast milk also changes consistency – in hot weather it becomes more thirst-quenching, so breast-fed babies don't need water between feeds. The milk even takes on different flavours from foods the mother eats, and this helps prepare babies for tastes they will come across later.

After a feed, hold your baby upright against your shoulder and gently rub their back to help release any trapped wind.

Why is it good for you?

Breast-feeding helps the womb contract following birth and may help you lose weight gained during pregnancy. It also reduces the risk of early breast or ovarian cancers, and osteoporosis (brittle bones) in later life. Breast-feeding produces the hormone prolactin, which has a calming effect, helping you relax during feeds. Breast-milk is always the right consistency for your baby, and needs no packaging or other resources. It is safe, convenient, hygienic and free.

Did you know?

Some studies have shown that breast-fed babies are less likely to become obese in childhood and are more likely to stay a healthy weight later in life.

Bottle-feeding

Manufactured baby milk, which is usually called 'infant formula', provides an alternative to breast milk or can be used alongside breast-feeding. Formula milk can't exactly match the composition of breast milk (as it doesn't contain antibodies, for example) but in terms of nutrition it will provide a healthy start for your baby as long as you prepare the milk following the manufacturer's instructions. Other kinds of milk are not suitable for babies under a year old.

Safety point

Don't forget to wash and dry your hands before preparing bottle feeds and before feeding your baby.

What is formula milk?

Formula milk is made from cow's milk that is modified by adjusting carbohydrate, protein and fat levels and adding vitamins and minerals essential for the growth and development of a baby. It comes in powder form, or ready-made in cartons which are particularly useful for journeys and emergencies. Most manufacturers make first- and second-stage milk. First-stage is most like breast milk, so should be used in the first six months. Second-stage (often called 'follow-on') milk has extra vitamins and minerals, especially iron, which babies need from six months.

There is a wide range of bottles and teats available.

Equipment

You'll need at least six bottles and teats for a fully bottle-fed baby. There's a huge variety to choose from, but newborn babies need small bottles and faster flowing teats as they become tired very quickly if they have to suck hard to make the milk flow. Teats and bottles must be sterilized. To do this, wash them thoroughly in warm, soapy water, rinse carefully in clean water and then sterilize using one of the methods described on the left. Alternatively, you can wash and sterilize feeding equipment in a dishwasher on a hot programme (at least 80°C/180°F).

Sterilization methods

• Steam sterilization using a plug-in electric sterilizer

• Steam sterilization using a sterilizer designed for use in a microwave

• Cold water sterilization using chemical sterilizing fluid or sterilizing tablets

• Sterilization by boiling the equipment for 10 minutes (3 minutes for teats) in a pan of tap water

Preparing feeds

When making milk from powder, use boiled tap water that has been allowed to cool for no more than half an hour. Add it to the bottle first (before the powder) as this helps ensure you use exactly the right amount.

Shake the bottle and test a few drops of the milk on the inside of your wrist before you start feeding. It should not feel hot or cool. If it is too hot, hold the bottle under a cool running tap, or warm the bottle by putting it in a container of warm water for a few minutes. Don't give your baby milk that has been kept warm though, as germs breed fast in warm milk.

Make sure your baby is somewhere safe while you are preparing feeds.

Feeding time

New babies have tiny stomachs so need a lot of small feeds and you will soon learn to recognize when your baby is hungry. They'll let you know when they're full, too, so don't force your baby to finish a bottle. Throw away any milk that's left after a feed as bacteria from the baby's saliva will live and breed in the warm liquid. You can find links to websites which give more advice and information about bottle-feeding on the Usborne Quicklinks Website (see page 91).

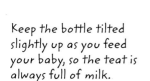

Keep the bottle tilted slightly up as you feed your baby, so the teat is always full of milk.

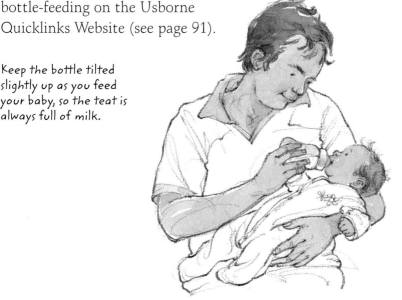

Safety point

It's dangerous to warm a baby's bottle in a microwave as the heat distribution in the milk may be uneven.

Allergic to milk?

• If you think your baby may be allergic to, or intolerant of, formula milk, talk to your doctor or health visitor.

• Babies may be prescribed 'hydrolysed' milk formula which has been modified for babies with milk allergy.

• Seek professional advice before giving babies non-dairy, soya-based formula as this can trigger a reaction too.

• Goat's milk formulas and follow-on formulas based on goat's milk protein are not suitable and have not been approved for use (in Europe).

Getting ready for weaning

Babies are born with a supply of iron stored in their livers, but by the time they are six months old, this supply begins to run low, so they need to start getting iron from food. While breast milk (or formula milk) will still provide most of their nutritional needs, from six months you can gradually start to introduce some 'solid' food into your baby's diet in the process known as weaning. If you feel that your baby is ready to start on solids earlier than six months, talk to your health visitor first. There are certain foods that should not be introduced before six months and introducing solids too early can contribute to over-feeding and may result in food allergies.

Equipment you need

A food processor or blender is the easiest way to make first foods for babies. These enable you to turn most foods into smooth purées that babies can swallow and digest easily. A hand-held electric blender is useful for making small amounts and is easy to clean. Some foods just need to be mashed with a fork. Whatever method you use, you are likely to make more food than you need and ice-cube trays are useful for freezing and storing the excess (see page 27).

Steaming food helps it to retain vitamins and minerals and is a good way of cooking vegetables for the whole family, so a collapsible steamer that fits into different sizes of pan, or an electric steamer, is also useful.

Equipment for making and storing baby food. (You can use a metal sieve with a lid on top if you don't have a steamer.)

Ready for weaning?

Signs that your baby may be ready for more than just milk include:

• Wanting more milk feeds than before.

• Showing signs of still being hungry after their milk feed.

• Waking up in the night for a feed again after starting to sleep through.

• Showing an interest in what you and other people eat – trying to grab food for example.

Equipment for feeding

Shallow weaning spoons with no hard edges

Heat-proof weaning bowls with a hand grip

Several soft, plastic-backed bibs

Safety point

All feeding equipment must be washed thoroughly, but you don't need to sterilize feeding spoons and bowls when your baby is six months and older.

6 – 8 months

By six months, many babies have begun to notice people around them eating and may be keen to try 'solid' food themselves. They need to be introduced to new foods one by one, first as semi-liquid purées and in tiny quantities. If all the advice about what babies can and can't have at different stages sounds complicated, the information in the following chapters is brought together in the chart on pages 88 and 89.

At a glance

How and when to feed first meals
and how much to feed

How to prepare first fruit and vegetable purées

What not to add to home-made baby foods

How to store home-made baby foods

Recipes for meat and fish dishes, casseroles,
stews and desserts

Drinks for your baby from six months

1. Get the food ready, wash your hands, then sit your baby on your lap, supporting their shoulders with one arm.

2. Dip your little finger into the food to test the temperature. If cool enough, let your baby suck some from your finger.

3. If this goes well, dip the tip of a spoon in the purée and place it between your baby's lips. Let them suck the food.

It takes time to learn how to take food from a spoon.

Foods for weaning

Home-made, single-ingredient fruit or vegetable purées or baby cereals (such as baby rice) are ideal first weaning foods. At first babies will be learning to take food from a spoon, so just offer small amounts thinned with breast or formula milk. It's a good idea to introduce new foods one at a time to start with; this will help you to recognize any allergic reactions to new foods (see pages 78 to 79 for more about food allergies) and it gently eases your baby into accepting new tastes and textures.

First feeds

Making children feel at ease when they're eating is one of the keys to getting them to eat well. You want your baby to be relaxed when feeding, so don't wait until they are crying with hunger or very tired when introducing first or new foods. Let them have a formula- or breast-milk feed first (and possibly afterwards if they want it). Offer them just one small teaspoon of the 'solid' food, mixed with milk for the first few feeds, following the steps on the left.

Safety point

Always stay with your baby or toddler when they are eating to make sure they don't choke. See page 91 for what to do if a baby does start choking.

Go at your baby's pace

Remember that all babies are different. Some take to solids quickly; others take longer. Some seem to like everything they are offered; others need more time to accept new foods. At this stage, the main aim of feeding is to get your baby used to taking food from a spoon. Most of their nourishment still comes from breast or formula milk. The tips on the left may make the process easier for you both.

• Allow plenty of time for feeding, especially at first, and go at your baby's pace. Babies need time to learn how to move the food to the back of their mouths and to swallow it.

• Don't spend ages trying to persuade babies to eat something they don't want and never try to force them to eat. If they really don't want the food, wait until the next time.

If you are weaning using baby rice, follow the instructions on the packet carefully and keep the mixture very thin to make swallowing easier for your baby.

Try to make mealtimes relaxed, unhurried and enjoyable from the start.

Apple or pear purée

• 1 dessert apple or pear (peeled, cored and sliced)
• a little water, formula or breast milk

Ripe pears and apples are good foods for weaning.

This is an ideal first purée. Use a ripe dessert apple or pear and taste a piece before cooking to make sure it's naturally sweet. First purées should be the consistency of runny yogurt once you have added milk or water.

1. Place the apple or pear slices in a metal sieve or steamer and gently steam for 8–10 minutes over a pan of boiling water with a lid on top.
2. Remove the pan from the heat and allow to cool.
3. When still just warm, mash the fruit to a purée in a small bowl using a fork.
4. To make the fruit into a thin purée that's easier for your baby to swallow, add some breast milk or formula milk or some of the water used for steaming.

Foods for first purées

- apples
- pears
- papayas
- melons
- bananas
- avocados
- carrots
- sweet potatoes
- butternut squash
- potatoes
- yams
- swedes
- parsnips
- broccoli

Ingredients for One-vegetable purée

- 1 carrot, parsnip, sweet potato or yam (washed, peeled and cut into small pieces)
- a little water, formula or breast milk

More first foods

Over the first few days of weaning, introduce a variety of purées or baby cereals one at a time. If your baby is having three milk feeds during the day, at times which equate to breakfast, lunch and an evening meal, offer a small amount of a different food at each of these times. You could try some sweet root vegetables such as carrots, parsnips or yams, following the recipe below. Ripe, mashed banana or avocado make 'instant' baby foods as neither needs to be cooked. Potatoes, sweet potatoes and chunks of butternut squash can all be baked in a hot oven (see page 42) or microwaved instead of steamed, and this retains more of their nutrients. When cooked, scoop out the flesh, mash, and add breast or formula milk if needed.

One-vegetable purée

1. Put the vegetable pieces in a sieve or steamer and gently steam until tender.
2. Remove the pan from the heat and allow to cool.
3. Whiz the food in a processor or blender.
4. Add some breast milk or formula milk, or some of the water used for steaming, to make a thin purée.

Carrot, parsnip and broccoli purées (before thinning)

Moving onto mixtures

It's important that babies get used to a good variety of sweet and savoury flavours during weaning, so after a few days, if your baby has had no adverse reactions to single purées, you can start to mix different foods together.

Mixed purées can be made from a combination of fruit and vegetables or can include baby cereals such as baby rice. It's vital to get good sources of iron into your baby foods. Fruit and vegetables that are rich in iron include green leafy vegetables such as spinach or broccoli, peas, green peppers, watercress, blackcurrants and mangoes. Dried fruit, beans and lentils provide iron too. Most fruit and vegetables are also good sources of other important nutrients such as vitamins A and C and folic acid.

Ideas for mixed purées

- *apple and carrot*
- *apple and apricot*
- *pear and peach*
- *pea and potato*
- *carrot and parsnip*
- *pea, carrot and parsnip*
- *beetroot and butternut squash*
- *courgette, apple and broccoli*

Try making mixed purées from a range of fruit and vegetables. If you use peas and beans, remove the skins by passing the purée through a sieve.

Storing purées

One apple, carrot and potato will make several servings of fresh purée which you can store (before thinning) for a day in a sealed container in the refrigerator. As you probably won't want to spend your whole time cooking up tiny quantities of baby food, it's useful to be able to store some for longer. A good method is to put the extra purée from a freshly-made batch into ice-cube trays and freeze it. When frozen, empty the purée cubes into a freezer bag and label it. You can then just remove one or two cubes at a time and heat them in a pan or microwave to defrost the purée. Always make sure the food has heated all the way through and has cooled again before you feed it to your baby.

Safety points

Don't add any salt or sugar to your baby's food.

Don't give them honey until they are at least a year old.

Make sure food has cooled almost completely before serving it to your baby.

Throw away any food that your baby doesn't eat at the end of a meal and don't refreeze food that has already been frozen.

Fresh herbs can add extra flavour to your baby's food.

Mixed meals

After a couple of weeks of weaning, once your baby is used to taking various different purées from a spoon, and certainly by the time they are six and a half months old, you should introduce a greater variety of foods and start moving from runny purées to thicker purées and mashed foods. Good foods to introduce at this stage are pulses such as beans and lentils, fish, lean meat, well-cooked eggs, yogurt and soft cheese. Babies who start weaning at six months will soon be able to manage mashed foods and it is important they start to learn to chew and accept lumps at this stage as this will help with their speech development.

Ingredients for Butter bean casserole

- 1 medium carrot (peeled and chopped)
- 1 small apple (peeled, cored and sliced)
- 1 small can of butter beans
- leaves of 2 sprigs of parsley (chopped)

Butter bean casserole

Butter beans are a good source of protein, vitamins and minerals and their creamy texture often appeals to babies. Try to buy beans canned in water for this recipe. If you can only find beans in salted water, make sure you rinse them thoroughly before you use them.

1. Put the carrot, apple and parsley into a steamer or metal sieve and steam over a pan of boiling water until soft.
2. Remove from the heat and allow to cool.
3. Drain and rinse the butter beans.
4. Mash all the ingredients together with a fork and add a little of the steaming liquid, or breast or formula milk.

Useful tip

You may be able to buy beans that have been canned without added salt or sugar in health food shops.

Ingredients for butter bean casserole

Cheesy leeks and potato

Ingredients for Cheesy leeks and potato

- 1 small leek (washed and finely sliced)
- 1 medium potato (peeled and cut into small cubes)
- 1 bay leaf
- 1 teaspoon full-fat soft cheese

This recipe introduces your baby to the mild, oniony taste of leeks. Use only the white part of the leek and make sure you wash it thoroughly under running water to remove any traces of dirt before cooking.

1. Put the leek, potato and bay leaf in a pan of water, bring to the boil and simmer until the potato is soft.
2. Remove from the heat, drain the vegetables and allow them to cool.
3. Remove the bay leaf and mash the vegetables together with the cheese.

You could also use leeks and potatoes to make some soup for the rest of the family.

Foods to avoid

- Unpasteurized milk and cheeses
- Raw or undercooked egg
- Honey
- Food with added salt, sugar or artificial sweeteners
- Babies with a history of food allergy, asthma, eczema or hayfever in the family should not have peanuts (and no child under five can have whole nuts).

Lentils with spinach

Ingredients for Lentils with spinach

- 55g (2oz) red lentils (rinsed)
- 1 medium carrot (peeled and finely chopped)
- 55g (2oz) spinach (washed and chopped)

Red lentils are quite quick to cook and are a good source of protein, iron and zinc. Remove any discoloured lentils or stones, and rinse the lentils in a sieve before you start.

1. Bring the lentils to the boil in a saucepan of water and simmer for about 15 minutes, or until they have softened completely.
2. Add the carrot to the saucepan along with the spinach, and cook for a further 5 minutes.
3. When the vegetables are soft, remove from the heat, drain and allow to cool before mashing with a fork. Add formula or breast milk to reach the right consistency.

Fish and meat meals

It's important to introduce good sources of iron into your baby's diet from six months, and the most easily absorbed form is found in meat and fish. You can ensure that babies get enough without eating these foods, but if they are part of your family's diet, there's no reason not to include them in meals. (See pages 76 and 77 for information on vegetarian diets.) Food hygiene is essential when cooking meat and fish, so follow the rules on the left and make sure food is cooked all the way through before serving.

Fish and meat are an important source of iron.

Salmon fishcakes

Ingredients for
Salmon fishcakes
(makes 8)

• 450g (1lb) potatoes (peeled)
• 2 slices of slightly stale bread
• 2 salmon fillets, each about 175g (6oz)
• black pepper
• juice of half a lemon
• some chopped parsley

Fishcakes can make a healthy meal for the whole family. They can be made in advance and kept in the refrigerator overnight or in the freezer for several weeks.

1. Boil the potatoes until soft, drain and mash.
2. Blitz the bread in a blender to make breadcrumbs.
3. Place the salmon fillets on a piece of oiled foil, squeeze over the lemon juice and sprinkle with pepper.
4. Cook the fillets under a medium grill for about 5 minutes on each side or until cooked through.
5. Set the oven to 200°C, 400°F or gas mark 6.
6. Flake the cooked salmon with a fork checking thoroughly for bones. Throw away the skin.
7. Stir the salmon and parsley into the mashed potatoes. When cool enough to handle, take out a spoonful of the mixture at a time and shape into a fishcake.
8. Coat in the breadcrumbs, place onto a warmed baking tray and bake the fishcakes in the oven for 20 minutes or until golden brown.

Mash half of a cooked fishcake up again before serving it to your baby.

Lamb couscous

Couscous is a useful cereal for baby food as it is very quick to prepare and is high in iron. Make sure that the lamb is cooked until it is very tender so you can mash it with the vegetables and couscous rather than having to purée it.

Ingredients for Lamb couscous (4 baby portions)

- 55g (2oz) couscous
- 125g (4oz) lean lamb, diced
- 200ml (¹/₃ pint) cold water
- 1 small carrot (peeled and chopped)
- 1 small stick of celery (chopped)
- 55g (2oz) canned chickpeas (drained and rinsed)
- sprig of parsley (chopped)

1. Soak the couscous in water for 5 minutes and then drain.
2. Put the lamb and the cold water into a saucepan and bring to the boil.
3. Simmer for 10 minutes and then add the carrot, celery, chickpeas and parsley.
4. Simmer for a further 5 minutes, or until all the ingredients are very soft.
5. Stir in the couscous, take off the heat and allow to cool.
6. Mash everything together with a fork.

Chicken and barley stew

Pearl barley is easy to digest and adds a slightly nutty flavour to this chicken stew.

Ingredients for Chicken and barley stew (4 baby portions)

- 55g (2oz) pearl barley
- 1 chicken fillet (skinned)
- a handful of parsley (chopped)
- 1 medium carrot (peeled and sliced)
- 1 stick of celery (chopped)

1. Soak the barley in cold water for 30 minutes.
2. Place the chicken in a saucepan and cover with water.
3. Bring to the boil and simmer for 20 minutes.
4. Take the chicken out of the saucepan and cut the meat into small pieces.
5. Return the meat to the saucepan and add the parsley, carrot, celery and barley.
6. Bring to the boil, reduce the heat and simmer for 30 minutes or until the barley has softened.
7. Mash everything with a fork when cooled.

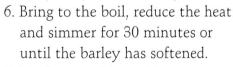

You don't have to cut the carrots and celery too small as they will be mashed.

Make sure the stew is cool before feeding it to your baby.

Drinks from six months

Although breast or formula milk should be your baby's main drink during the whole of their first year, from six months other drinks can start to play a part in their feeding routine. As soon as babies start eating solids, they can start drinking water and this is a good habit to get children into, as water is the best alternative drink to milk. Most babies will still be having three or four milk drinks a day (600 to 800ml or 1 to 1⅓ pints) as well as food at mealtimes, but milk is the only drink that should be given in a bottle.

You can give your baby water in addition to breast or formula milk from six months.

Safety point

Some bottled waters are unsuitable for babies due to high levels of calcium and sodium. Check the label before giving bottled water to your baby or toddler.

Drinks from 6 to 12 months

• Breast milk or follow-on (second stage) formula milk

• Tap water (where it's safe to drink) or some types of bottled water (see above)

• Diluted fresh fruit juice – one part juice to ten parts water

Did you know?

Tea and coffee should not be given to young children as they contain caffeine and tannins which reduce iron absorption.

Any drink with sugar added to it can cause tooth decay.

Any fizzy drink or fruit-based drink (even if it has no added sugar) can erode baby tooth enamel.

From bottle to beaker

From about six months, start offering your baby water or milk in a cup between meals. It's a good idea to wean babies off drinking from bottles entirely by the time they are one. This is because bottle-sucking can become a habit that is hard to break, and using a teat means that the milk is in continuous contact with their emerging teeth, which increases the risk of tooth decay. Try a 'free-flow' lidded beaker, an open beaker or a cup which your baby can learn to sip from, rather than the kind which requires them to suck (such as non-spill cups with valves).

About fruit drinks

From six months you can offer your baby diluted fresh fruit juice in a cup with meals. This provides a source of vitamin C which helps them absorb iron from their food. Only use 100 per cent pure fruit juice (not 'juice drinks') and dilute one part juice to ten parts tap water. Squashes or any other drinks aren't suitable as they may contain artificial sweeteners. Even many of the various products sold as baby drinks (for example herb drinks) are high in sugar which can damage teeth. There's no reason to give your baby any drinks other than diluted juice with meals, formula or breast milk, or water.

Different kinds of milk

When your baby is a year old, you can gradually start replacing formula or breast milk with full-fat cow's milk. A one-year old should drink about 600ml (1 pint) of milk a day. You can introduce semi-skimmed milk after the age of two, as long as the rest of your child's diet is varied and healthy. Skimmed milk isn't suitable as a main drink until children are five as it doesn't contain enough calories for a growing child. Flavoured milk also isn't suitable as it contains added sugar.

Full-fat goat's or sheep's milk can be given once a baby is a year old, as long as it is pasteurized. (Pasteurization involves heating to kill bacteria.) Soya milk doesn't contain the range of nutrients provided by full-fat cow's milk, so if you use it, choose brands with added vitamins, particularly calcium, or use fortified soya formula. Give soya milk in a cup, not a bottle.

Don't leave babies to feed alone, even when they can hold their own bottles.

Milk allergy

- *About five per cent of babies have milk allergies but most grow out of them by the time they are three.*

- *Allergic reactions can vary from relatively mild to extremely serious.*

- *Reactions include skin rashes, diarrhoea, vomiting, stomach cramps and (very rarely) difficulty in breathing.*

- *Find out more about food intolerance and allergies on pages 78 to 79.*

All kinds of fruit can be used to make baby desserts.

Fruity desserts

You can make a variety of sweet dishes for babies using fruit purées mixed with various cereals or yogurt. You could start by using baby rice or baby porridge as a base and introduce a new flavour of fruit purée or a compote (page 38). If this goes down well, you could try mixing a fruit purée with some full-fat natural yogurt, rice pudding or some semolina.

Apricot semolina

Apricots provide carbohydrates and fibre, vitamins A and C and also the minerals calcium, potassium and iron.

Ingredients for Apricot semolina

- 100g (3 1/2 oz) canned or fresh apricots (cut in half and stones removed)
- 300ml (1/2 pint) water
- 4 teaspoons semolina
- 4 teaspoons full-fat cow's milk

1. Place the apricots in a saucepan, cover with the water and bring to the boil. Simmer until tender.
2. Blend the apricots in a liquidizer with the cooking water until you have a smooth purée.
3. Put the semolina and milk in a pan. Heat slowly, stirring all the time until thickened. Remove from the heat.
4. Stir in 2 teaspoons of the apricot purée (or another fruit purée of your choice).

Mix the apricot purée into the semolina, or just swirl some on top.

Choose apricots canned in juice, not syrup, for this recipe.

9 – 11 months

From nine months your baby should be eating three meals
a day as well as some healthy snacks in between. During this
stage, babies start to reduce their milk intake and move onto
minced or chopped foods. They may now have their first teeth
and need to learn to chew and also to take a more active role
in feeding themselves. It's important that your baby now
starts to take part in family meals and eats some
of the same foods as the rest of the family.

At a glance

How to encourage growing appetites by introducing
lots of new tastes and textures

Moving from puréed and mashed food to chopped or
minced meals to encourage chewing

Recipes for baby breakfasts and main meals

Getting children interested in feeding themselves by
offering finger foods with different textures

New ingredients

• More dairy products such as full-fat hard cheese, yogurt or fromage frais

• Full-fat cow's milk on cereal and in cooking (but formula or breast milk still main drink)

• More fresh or canned oily fish (always check for bones)

• More eggs (must be well cooked and not runny or raw)

• Stronger flavours such as herbs, onions, garlic, olives and sweet peppers

• Tiny quantities of milder spices such as black pepper, cinnamon and ginger

Remember to brush baby teeth twice a day with a soft baby toothbrush and a little bit of fluoride toothpaste.

Safety point

Make sure your baby sits upright in a highchair at mealtimes. If they are scrunched up or leaning backwards in a buggy or car seat while feeding, they can choke easily.

Growing appetites

Once the early weeks of weaning are over, most babies enjoy sampling new tastes and develop a good appetite for solids. By the time they are toddlers, however, many start to assert very specific likes and dislikes and may refuse to try new foods, so it's important to make the most of this appetite 'window'. Research shows that if a child has been introduced to a wide range of foods straight from weaning, they're more likely to accept them, so now is the time to introduce new flavours and textures and make meals as varied and interesting as possible.

Keep serving familiar foods too, but adjust the texture and combine with new ingredients. Food can now be grated, chopped or minced, rather than puréed, and you can offer finger foods (see page 44) for chewing practice. Your baby should still be having breast milk or about 600 to 800ml (1 to 1⅓ pints) of formula or follow-on formula milk a day.

Foods for teething

The time babies get their first teeth varies – some babies are born with a tooth or two – but most will have at least two teeth by nine months and they may dribble, gnaw and be fussier than usual about their food when teething. Some carrot, celery or cucumber sticks that have been chilled in the refrigerator can help to soothe sore gums (but keep a close eye on babies at all times when they are chewing them).

Peel cucumbers and carrots before cutting them into sticks.

Dairy products

Dairy products such as cheese, yogurt and fromage frais are good sources of protein, calcium, phosphorus and riboflavin and can all be included in your baby's diet. It's best to avoid fruit yogurts and other flavoured yogurts as these often contain a lot of sugar. Instead, buy natural yogurt or fromage frais and add your own fruit, fruit purée or compote (see page 38). Hard cheese contains a lot of salt, so only use it in small quantities to flavour dishes for your baby. Cottage cheese and soft (cream) cheese are generally lower in salt. Remember to make sure your baby always has full-fat dairy products, as they need an energy- and nutrient-dense diet while they are growing rapidly.

Fibre facts

Remember that while adults and older children should be eating a diet which contains plenty of fibre-rich foods, this is not recommended for children under the age of five. Foods which are very high in fibre, such as some breakfast cereals, breads, brown rice and wholewheat pasta can fill up small stomachs easily.

Babies need nutrient-dense foods and, while they need some fibre in their diets to prevent constipation, it is better that they have more soluble fibre from fruit and vegetables, particularly foods such as peas, beans and pulses, green leafy vegetables and soft fruits such as berries, grapes, apricots and plums.

Foods to avoid

• *Don't add salt to your baby's food or give them any foods with added salt.*

• *Limit sugar to the small amount you need to add to sour foods such as some fruits.*

• *Avoid artificial sweeteners found in fruit squashes, diet food and drinks.*

• *Don't give foods which carry a risk of food-poisoning, such as soft, mould-ripened or unpasteurized cheeses.*

• *Avoid honey, liver pâté and raw or lightly cooked eggs.*

• *Don't give whole nuts, and avoid peanuts if there is a family history of allergies.*

Babies can get the fibre they need from fruit and vegetables.

Fruity porridge

Ingredients for
Fruity porridge
(for 2 adults and a baby)

- 1 cup porridge oats
- 2 cups full-fat cow's milk or formula milk
- 1 tablespoon mixed berry compote or fruit purée

Porridge is easy to make for breakfast and oats are a good source of fibre and B vitamins. As long as you don't add any salt or sugar, your baby can have the same porridge as the rest of the family.

1. Tip the oats into a saucepan and stir in the milk.
2. Heat slowly, stirring regularly.
3. Once thickened to the consistency you and your baby prefer, remove from the heat.
4. Stir in berry compote (see below), fruit purée or one of the things listed on the left.

More good things to add to porridge

- _mashed banana and a quarter teaspoon of ground cinnamon_
- _a tablespoon of apricot purée (see page 34)_
- _some chopped dried fruit_
- _a teaspoon of maple syrup_

Let porridge cool before feeding it to your baby.

Mixed berry compote

Ingredients for
Mixed berry compote

- 450g (1lb) fresh or frozen berries
- 2 tablespoons caster sugar
- 3 tablespoons water

A fruit compote can be used as a dessert, added to porridge, yogurt and milk puddings, or served on pancakes. Berries contain high levels of antioxidants which may help boost children's immunity. They can be expensive out of season, but if you buy or pick at the right time, you could make a big batch of compote and freeze some. Use any kind of berry, or a combination such as raspberries, blackberries, blackcurrants, redcurrants and strawberries.

Use the ice-cube tray method described on page 27 to freeze small quantities.

1. Remove any stalks and leaves before putting the berries in a heavy-bottomed saucepan with the sugar and water.
2. Warm gradually on a low heat. Allow to reach simmering point and remove from the heat when the skins begin to burst. Allow to cool before serving with porridge, etc.

Useful eggs

Eggs are a very versatile food for babies and toddlers and contain protein, iron, vitamin A and vitamin D. They must be cooked until both the white and yolk are solid, and it's also important to buy free-range eggs or those guaranteed to come from a salmonella-free flock. For breakfast, eggs can be served hard boiled in slices, scrambled, fried or in 'eggy bread' (see page 54).

There are more ideas for using eggs on pages 54 and 55.

Scrambled eggs

Scrambled eggs make a quick main meal or breakfast for babies and toddlers and you can adapt this recipe easily by adding one of the things listed below, on the left. Add a tiny bit of black pepper (but no salt) for extra flavour.

1. Carefully crack the eggs into a bowl and beat them well with a fork. Add the pepper.
2. Put the butter in a pan over a medium heat and, when it starts to foam, add the eggs.
3. Stir frequently with a wooden spoon to stop the eggs from sticking.
4. Take the pan off the heat when the eggs are no longer runny, but not overcooked.

Ingredients for Scrambled eggs

- 2 eggs
- knob of unsalted butter
- ground black pepper

Good things to add to scrambled eggs

- a tablespoon of finely grated cheddar cheese
- a tablespoon of full-fat cottage cheese
- some chopped fresh herbs and a finely chopped tomato
- a finely sliced spring onion, cooked in butter until soft
- 2 finely chopped button mushrooms

You could sprinkle fresh herbs such as chopped chives on scrambled eggs.

Creamy pea and Parmesan risotto

Risotto has a soft, creamy texture and is easy for babies to eat. This recipe makes enough for a family meal with the risotto as a side dish or starter for the adults. You could stir in chopped tomato, spinach or broccoli instead of the peas.

1. Heat the oil in a heavy-bottomed saucepan, add the onion and fry until soft.
2. Add the rice and stir until it begins to go translucent.
3. Gradually add the water, a little at a time, stirring until it has been absorbed by the rice.
4. Cook for about 35 minutes in total, stirring regularly.
5. When the rice is soft, add the peas and warm through.
6. Remove from the heat and stir in the cheese and parsley.

Ingredients for Pea and Parmesan risotto (for 2 adults and a baby)

- half a tablespoon olive oil
- half a small onion (peeled and chopped)
- 100g (3 ½ oz) Arborio rice
- 300ml (½ pint) water
- 55g (2oz) fresh or frozen peas
- 30g (1oz) Parmesan cheese (grated)
- 1 teaspoon fresh parsley (chopped)

Rice and red lentils

Red lentils are a good source of protein, fibre and iron. This is a colourful meal that older children may like as well.

1. Rinse the rice and lentils in a sieve and place in a saucepan with the water.
2. Bring to the boil, reduce heat and simmer for 20 minutes.
3. Fry the onion in the olive oil until soft. Add the tomatoes, carrots, peas and peppers and cook until soft.
4. Stir in the lentils and rice. Remove from heat.

Ingredients for Rice and red lentils (6 baby servings)

- 30g (1oz) long grain white rice
- 85g (3oz) red lentils
- 450ml (¾ pint) water
- 1 teaspoon olive oil
- 1 small onion (finely chopped)
- 200g (7oz) canned tomatoes (chopped)
- quarter of a red pepper (finely diced)
- 1 small carrot (peeled and finely diced)
- handful of peas
- 1 teaspoon fresh parsley (finely chopped)

Sprinkle on chopped parsley and serve the rice and red lentils when it has cooled a little.

Red pepper and tomato rice

Ingredients for
Red pepper and tomato rice
(4 baby servings)

- 1 medium red pepper
  (finely chopped)
- 2 teaspoons olive oil
- 2 tomatoes (finely diced)
- half a clove of garlic (crushed)
- 100g (3½ oz) Arborio rice
- 200ml (⅓ pint) water
- sprig of parsley (chopped)

Red peppers are a very good source of vitamins A and C and have a sweet taste and an appearance which usually appeals to babies and toddlers. There is no need to skin peppers for cooked dishes; just cut them in half, remove the stalk, seeds and core, and chop the pepper finely.

1. Heat the oil in a saucepan and add the tomatoes, chopped peppers and the garlic. Cook for 2 minutes.
2. Add the rice and water and bring to the boil.
3. Reduce the heat and simmer for about 20 minutes until all the water is absorbed and the rice is tender.
4. Allow to cool and serve sprinkled with parsley.

You could let your baby play with another red pepper while you are cooking this recipe.

Mini pasta and fresh pesto

Ingredients for
Mini pasta and fresh pesto

- 2 small handfuls of mini
  pasta shapes per baby
- 55g (2oz) fresh basil leaves
- half a clove of garlic
- 30g (1oz) pine nuts
- 4 tablespoons olive oil
- 2 tablespoons Parmesan
  cheese (grated)
- 2 teaspoons lemon juice

Pesto sauce is a useful standby and rich in nutrients. You can buy it ready-made, though jars of pesto are often high in salt. If you can get fresh basil, it's easy to make and will last in the refrigerator for a few weeks in a sealed jar. You only need a half teaspoon of pesto per serving for babies as it has a strong, rich flavour.

1. Put the basil, garlic, pine nuts and half the oil into a blender and whiz into a smooth paste.
2. Pour the paste into a jar and stir in the rest of the oil, Parmesan cheese and lemon juice.
3. Bring a pan of water to the boil and cook the pasta following the instructions on the packet. Drain and stir in a half teaspoon of the pesto for each portion.

Little cheesy baked potato

**Ingredients for
Little cheesy baked potato
(for 1 baby)**

- 1 small baking potato
- 30g (1oz) cheese (grated)
- 1 small tomato
  (finely diced)

**Other good things to mix
with baked potato**

- a spoonful of cottage cheese
- a little cream cheese and
  some chopped chives
- a little flaked, canned
  tuna, mixed with
  natural yogurt

This is a very simple dish to prepare as long as you remember to put the potato in the oven well over an hour before you plan to eat (to allow for cooling time too). As you are heating the oven for this length of time, you may want to make enough potatoes for a family meal, rather than just one. If you can, use organic potatoes, scrub them and prick the skins with a fork or push metal skewers through them to stop the skins from bursting in the oven. Baked potatoes are also delicious served with a tablespoon of home-made baked beans (recipe opposite).

1. Cook the potato in a hot oven at 220°C, 425°F or gas mark 7, for about 50 minutes (or until soft all the way through when you spike it with a skewer).
2. Remove from the oven using oven gloves and allow to cool. (This will take at least 20 minutes.)
3. Cut an oval 'lid' in the potato, scoop out the contents, and mix it with the cheese and tomato.
4. Put the contents back into the potato skin and serve.

Add some vegetable finger foods such as green beans to balance this meal.

Cheese, leek and potato bake

Ingredients for
Cheese, leek and potato bake
(2 baby servings)

• 2 medium potatoes (peeled)
• white part of half a small leek
(washed and thinly sliced)
• 30g (1oz) cheese (grated)
• 1 teaspoon parsley (chopped)
• 6 tablespoons full-fat milk

This makes enough for two little portions, but if you up the quantities, it can work well as a light family meal.

1. Heat the oven to 160°C, 325°F or gas mark 3.
2. Parboil the potatoes whole in a saucepan of water for 10 minutes.
3. Remove from the heat, drain and allow the potatoes to cool a little. Slice them thinly.
4. Layer the potato, leeks, cheese and parsley in a small oven-proof dish, topping with a final layer of potato.
5. Pour over the milk.
6. Cook in the oven for 50 minutes, or until the potatoes are cooked through and the bake is golden brown on top.

You will need to chop up the pototoes on your baby's plate before serving.

Keep the dish well out of the reach of children as it will be very hot.

Home-made baked beans

Ingredients for
Home-made baked beans
(5 baby servings)

• 1 teaspoon olive oil
• 1 small onion (finely chopped)
• 4 medium tomatoes
(chopped)
• half a small eating apple
(peeled, cored and
quartered)
• 150ml (¼ pint) water
• 400g (14oz) can haricot
beans (drained)
• 1 teaspoon chopped parsley

Look for haricot beans canned with no added salt for this recipe. Alternatively, you could soak a couple of handfuls of dried haricot beans overnight in cold water and then boil them until very soft before adding them at step 6. Home-made baked beans can be stored for a day or two in a sealed container in the refrigerator.

1. Heat the oil in a heavy-bottomed saucepan, add the onion and fry until soft.
2. Add the tomatoes, apple and water.
3. Bring to the boil and allow to reduce for 5 minutes.
4. Remove from the heat, add the parsley and leave to cool for a few minutes.
5. Mash up the mixture with a fork or potato masher.
6. Return to the pan and stir in the haricot beans.
7. Cook on a low heat for 10 minutes until beans are soft.

Finger foods

- steamed green beans
- steamed broccoli pieces
- steamed carrot sticks
- fingers of cheese
- chunks of banana
- pieces of soft pear
- pieces of strawberry
- chunks of melon
- cucumber sticks
- pieces of peeled apple
- raw carrot sticks
- unsalted rice cakes
- breadsticks
- fingers of toast
- strips of pitta bread
- cooked pasta shapes

Finger foods

By nine to 11 months, babies can hold and chew on a variety of foods and you can encourage them to eat more independently by offering a range of finger foods. You could put a few things on their highchair tray while you prepare a meal, or give finger food snacks between meals. Finger foods can either be soft in texture and easily chewed and swallowed, or firmer to provide babies with something to test their new teeth on. Avoid giving biscuits and rusks which contain sugar. Instead, try some of the ideas listed on the left, or the potato wedges below (which can also be a side dish for adults if you increase the quantities).

Picking up and holding finger foods helps babies develop their fine motor skills.

Ingredients for Potato wedges

- 1 medium potato
- 1 tablespoon olive oil

Serve potato wedges with tomato sauce (page 49) or some natural yogurt.

Potato wedges

1. Heat the oven to 200°C, 400°F or gas mark 6.
2. Scrub the potato and cut it into eight wedges.
3. Bring a saucepan of water to the boil and add the wedges.
4. Return to the boil and simmer for 5 minutes.
5. Drain the potato wedges and place them on a roasting tray and drizzle the olive oil over them.
6. Bake the wedges in the oven for around 30 minutes, turning every 10 minutes until they are golden brown.
7. Allow the wedges to cool, and serve when they are just warm. (Make sure you test a wedge for temperature before giving it to your baby.)

Toddler meals

From one year, toddlers can eat many of the same foods as the rest of the family. Just take out their portion before you add any seasoning and make sure there are no hard bones they could choke on. You can also start to give full-fat cow's milk as a main drink and toddlers will probably drink about 3 cups (300 to 450ml or ½ to ¾ pints) a day.

The recipes in this section are for family meals and make four adult servings (unless it says otherwise). There's advice about how much to give toddlers on page 65.

At a glance

Advice on encouraging good eating habits
and making mealtimes happy and enjoyable

Recipes for family food including healthy main meals,
salads, fish dishes, desserts, drinks and treats

What to do when toddlers refuse food,
and preventing 'fussy' eating

Information on snacking and
ideas for healthy snacks

Family food

By the age of one, most children can chew and swallow a wide variety of foods with different textures and tastes. They should be able to manage mashed food with lumps, chopped, grated and minced food and many finger foods. You can offer your child most of the foods that adults eat, just make sure that they are of good quality and are not highly processed and laden with salt or sugar.

A young toddler's diet should include all the main food groups (see page 10) in the proportions shown on the left. Offering a wide variety of foods is the most reliable way to make sure your child is getting all the nutrients they need for their healthy growth and development.

From one year, aim to give your child each day:

- 4 or 5 servings of starchy food (rice, bread, pasta, potatoes, etc.)
- At least 2 portions of fruit
- At least 3 portions of vegetables
- 2 servings of lean meat, fish, eggs or meat alternatives
- 2 or 3 servings of milk, cheese or yogurt

Lunch for a one-year old

Cook a handful of pasta (see page 48). Chop a tomato and fry gently in a teaspoon of olive oil. Stir in a tablespoon of canned flaked tuna together with a few leaves of finely chopped spinach. Mix into drained pasta and sprinkle with grated cheese.

For dessert, serve two tablespoons of natural yogurt with a spoonful of fruit compote (see page 38) or some mashed berries.

Give water or diluted fruit juice (see page 33) in a cup to drink during the meal. Offer breast milk or full-fat cow's milk to drink after the meal.

Make mealtimes fun

Children learn their initial eating habits and behaviour from those around them, so try to eat together around a table as much as possible and set a good example yourself. The best way to show that eating is an enjoyable activity is to make mealtimes happy and sociable occasions.

Don't expect too much too soon, however. It's unlikely that a toddler who doesn't want to sit still for more than five minutes will be able to sit for half an hour at a table. Remember that little children are 'programmed' to move around and play just about all the time. For them, a meal is just an interruption in (or extension of) their playtime, however much effort you have put into preparing the food. However, if you continue to set a good example and make meals fun and chatty, gradually children may want to stay at the table longer and join in more.

Eating with other people and seeing them eat a variety of foods may also help encourage children to try different foods themselves, and if older children are involved, this can inspire toddlers to mimic them and try harder to master the use of a spoon and fork.

Timing meals

Routine is important for babies and young children and they are more likely to behave and eat well if they are not over-hungry, tired or already full up with snacks and drinks. To prevent meltdowns, it's a good idea to try to organize mealtimes for about the same time every day, but don't feel you have to be a slave to routine. The occasional picnic, meal out in a child-friendly café or restaurant, or at a friend's home, can be exciting and an opportunity for your child to try new kinds of foods in a different setting.

Take a bag of toys and a few snacks when you eat out to keep toddlers amused while you wait.

A picnic, inside or outdoors, can provide a welcome change to mealtime routines.

Foods to avoid

• Whole nuts (ground or chopped can be used)
• Very hot or spicy foods
• Raw eggs or eggs with runny yolks
• Fizzy drinks and squashes
• Tea and coffee
• Unpasteurized milk
• Fish such as swordfish, shark or marlin

Foods to limit

• Salt
• Sugar
• Honey
• Jam or syrup added to food

Staying calm

In their second year, many toddlers start to refuse to eat new foods or foods they have liked before. However frustrating it is when your child rejects something you have lovingly prepared, try to remain calm and don't let mealtimes become a battleground. Children often lose their appetites completely if they are shouted at, pressurized into eating, rushed through a meal or forced to sit down and eat something. (There is more advice on how to prevent and deal with 'fussy' eating on pages 64 and 65.) Also, try to stay relaxed however much mess children make as they learn to feed themselves. For a while, just resign yourself to the fact you'll have to do a lot of cleaning up after meals.

Staying calm when your child makes a mess helps them to stay relaxed around food.

Spaghetti

Tagliatelli

Fusilli

Macaroni

Conchiglie

Ingredients for Macaroni cheese (serves 4)

- 225g (8oz) macaroni or small pasta shapes
- 1 tablespoon olive oil
- 30g (1oz) butter
- 55g (2oz) plain flour
- 900ml (1½ pints) milk
- 225g (8oz) cheddar cheese (grated)

Tips for pasta meals

- Stir pasta once when you have put it in the water and don't overcook it.

- Drain pasta well before adding sauce or topping.

- Many children like pasta with just a splash of olive oil or a sprinkling of cheese.

- Serve pasta with some salad or vegetables for a well balanced meal.

You could add a few peas to macaroni cheese for extra vitamins.

Pasta meals

Pasta, fresh or dried, is easy to cook as long as you use a large pan of boiling water and follow the instructions and timing on the pasta packet. There are lots of types to choose from, including mini-shapes and spaghetti which often appeal to toddlers.

Macaroni cheese

This toddler favourite can be turned into a 'gratin' with a crunchy top by adding fresh breadcrumbs to the cheese for the topping and sprinkling this mixture over the pasta at step 4. Grill until the crumbs begin to go brown.

1. Cook the macaroni in a large pan of boiling water following the timing on the packet.
2. Put the oil, butter, flour and milk in a pan and, using a hand whisk, beat over a medium heat until thickened. Remove from heat and add three-quarters of the cheese.
3. Drain the macaroni, return it to the pan and stir in the cheese sauce. Mix well.
4. Tip into an oven-proof dish. Sprinkle with the remaining cheese and put under a hot grill for 5 minutes or until the cheese begins to bubble.

Useful tomato sauce

There are many great Italian pasta sauces including this simple and very useful tomato sauce. It's worth making it in quantity and freezing some as it can also be used for pizza (page 50), or to accompany potato wedges (page 44), home-made fish fingers (page 59) or fishcakes (page 30), instead of sugary tomato ketchup.

1. Heat the oil in a frying pan and fry the onion and garlic until soft.
2. Add the tomatoes and chopped herbs (but if using basil, tear it by hand and add it at step 4). Stir well.
3. Just before the sauce boils, turn down the heat and cook for at least 30 minutes, stirring occasionally.
4. When cooled, either mash with a fork for a rough texture, or whiz in a blender for a smoother sauce (which children may prefer).

How much pasta?

Dried pasta — Use 30g to 55g (1oz to 2oz) per small child and 85g to 125g (3oz to 4oz) per adult.

Fresh pasta — Use 55g to 85g (2oz to 3oz) per small child and 125g to 155g (4oz to 5oz) per adult.

You could freeze small amounts of the sauce in plastic tubs.

Crème fraiche carbonara

This creamy sauce goes well with spaghetti or a 'ribbon' shaped pasta such as papardelle or tagliatelle. You could add some peas to the pasta a minute before it finishes cooking or some sliced mushrooms at the end of step 2.

1. Dry fry the bacon pieces until crisp. Remove from pan and place on a kitchen towel to remove any excess fat.
2. Heat the oil in a frying pan and gently cook the onion and garlic for 5 minutes until softened.
3. Add the crème fraiche, bacon and parsley to the pan and stir to heat through.
4. Pour this sauce over cooked pasta. Sprinkle with the grated cheese.
5. Serve with a green salad.

Pizza dough

Shop-bought or takeaway pizzas are usually high in salt and fat, but if you make them yourself and control what goes into them, they can provide perfectly balanced meals for children. In this dough recipe, warm water is used to help activate the yeast. Don't be tempted to use hot water as this will kill the yeast, and don't be put off by what looks like a lot of steps; pizzas are easy and fun to make.

1. Put the flour, salt and yeast into a bowl and make a well in the middle. Pour in the warm water and oil.
2. Mix the ingredients into dough. If you need to add more water to get the dough to the right consistency, do this a drop at a time as it's easy to add too much.
3. Knead the dough for 10 minutes on a floured worktop.
4. Put the dough in a large bowl, cover with a clean towel or clingfilm and leave to rise in a warm, draft-free area for 1 hour or until doubled in size.
5. Divide the dough into 4 equal pieces and roll each one into a circle about 20cm (8in) across.
6. Place the bases on warm, oiled baking trays ready for topping or put in the refrigerator until you need them.

**Ingredients for
Pizza dough (serves 4)**

- 450g (1lb) strong flour
- 1 sachet of dried yeast
- 1 tablespoon olive oil
- 300ml (½ pint) warm water
- ¼ teaspoon salt

How to knead

- Roll up your sleeves and dust a worktop with flour.

- Using the heels of your hands, push the dough away from you, then fold it in half towards you.

- Turn it around and repeat again and again in rhythmic movements.

- Continue until the dough feels smooth and elastic.

Making pizzas

To make the pizzas, pre-heat the oven to 220°C, 425°F or gas mark 7, then spread a tablespoon of tomato sauce or passata on each base to about 1.5cm (½in) clear of the edge. You can use home-made tomato sauce (recipe on page 49), or ready-made passata (Italian tomato sauce) from a carton or bottle.

Add whatever toppings you want (there are some ideas on the opposite page) before sprinkling on about two tablespoons of grated cheese – a mixture of mozzarella and cheddar works well. Place the pizzas in the oven and cook on a high heat for about 12 minutes until the edges start to turn golden and the cheese begins to melt. Remember to let the pizza cool before you serve it to your toddler.

Use the back of a spoon to spread passata on the dough.

Balancing the meal

Pizza toppings can be a good way to introduce new foods and get children to eat vegetables, but if they'll only eat a tomato and cheese pizza, that's fine. The base provides carbohydrate, they'll get vitamins such as A and C from the tomato, and protein and calcium from the cheese. If you can get them to eat some fruit and salad too, they'll be eating a healthy meal.

Ideas for pizza toppings

- chopped ham
- cooked bacon pieces
- flakes of canned tuna
- olives (stoned and sliced)
- sweetcorn kernels
- cherry tomatoes (halved)
- sliced peppers
- mashed canned sardines (mash bones too for extra calcium)
- grated courgette
- pesto
- mushroom slices
- shredded spinach
- asparagus tips

Cheat's pizza

When there's no time to make dough, you could use a soft flour tortilla, a pitta bread, half an English muffin or half a small baguette as a pizza base. Place slices of tomato or a layer of tomato sauce on top and add whatever topping you want. Sprinkle with cheese and grill under a pre-heated grill at medium heat until the cheese is bubbling.

English muffin

Pitta bread

English muffins and pitta breads are both useful sources of starchy carbohydrate.

Pitta bread

You can also use the basic pizza dough on the opposite page to make pitta breads. Strips of pitta are great finger foods for babies and toddlers and can be dipped into hummus or cottage cheese for a healthy snack.

1. Pre-heat the oven to 220°C, 425°F or gas mark 7.
2. After the dough has risen (step 4 of pizza dough recipe), divide it into 10 pieces and form into flat ovals.
3. Place the ovals on warm, lightly oiled baking trays and cook in the oven for 10 minutes.

Salad ideas

Finger food salads

Finger food salads

- carrot sticks
- slices of red, yellow, green and orange pepper
- cucumber and celery sticks
- baby sweetcorn
- halved cherry tomatoes
- mange tout or sugar snap peas
- halved baby mushrooms
- chunks of avocado

Salads are packed with useful nutrients, and if you introduce them into a baby's diet as soon as the child is able to eat them, there is no reason they should be any less popular than other foods. Aim to serve a small portion of salad once or twice a day. Children are often attracted to the bright colours of raw vegetables, many of which make excellent finger foods. Toddlers often prefer having each food served separately on a plate, so plates which have dividing sections can be useful for offering different salad vegetables. You could try some of the ideas on the left.

Many children prefer their salad without any dressing (and for this age group dressings can add to the mess). However, reluctant salad-eaters can sometimes be encouraged to try something new if you serve their salad with a creamy dressing made from a tablespoon of full-fat natural yogurt, a few chopped chives and a squeeze of fresh orange juice. Alternatively you could try a dressing made from olive or sunflower oil and balsamic vinegar. (Balsamic vinegar has a sweet taste which often appeals to children.)

Salads can contribute to the goal of at least three servings of vegetables a day.

For a green salad, wash and tear up a few leaves of cos, romaine or round lettuce. Add sliced cucumber, and an oil and vinegar dressing if you want.

For bean salad, drain and rinse a can of flageolet, cannellini, borlotti or butter beans. Add chopped parsley, diced tomatoes and the juice of half an orange.

Crisp vegetable salad

Ingredients for Crispy vegetable salad (serves 4)

- 1 red and 1 yellow pepper
- 6 cherry tomatoes
- a quarter cucumber
- juice of half an orange

1. Cut the peppers in half and remove the seeds and cores. Slice the peppers thinly.
2. Cut the tomatoes in half. Slice the cucumber into matchstick length pieces.
3. Mix everything together and squeeze the juice over it.

Crunchy carrot salad

Ingredients for Crunchy carrot salad (serves 4)

- 4 medium carrots (washed and peeled)
- bunch of parsley (chopped)
- sunflower or olive oil
- vinegar or lemon juice

1. Grate the carrots into a bowl and add the parsley.
2. Stir in a splash of oil and a couple of splashes of vinegar or lemon juice. (Alternatively you could squeeze the juice of half an orange over the salad).

Salad Niçoise

Ingredients for Salad Niçoise (serves 4)

- 6 small new potatoes (scrubbed clean and cut into quarters)
- leaves of 1 round lettuce (washed, dried and torn up)
- 12 cherry tomatoes (halved)
- 55g (2oz) black olives (stoned and cut in half)
- 200g (8oz) can tuna steak (drained)
- 55g (2oz) green beans (washed and trimmed)
- 2 medium eggs
- oil and lemon juice for dressing

This classic French salad has a number of ingredients that toddlers usually enjoy, whether these are mixed together, or served separately. It is also a well balanced meal which looks lovely. Use fresh tuna (grilled and flaked) if you prefer.

1. Put the potatoes in a pan of water and bring to the boil.
2. Arrange the lettuce and tomatoes in a large bowl. Put the tuna and olives on top.
3. When the potatoes have cooked for 12 minutes, add the beans. Cook for 2 or 3 more minutes then drain.
4. Boil the eggs for 6–7 minutes. Drain and allow to cool.
5. Peel the eggs and cut them in quarters. Add the potatoes and beans and the eggs to the salad.
6. Drizzle adult portions with dressing (with finely chopped garlic or parsley in it if you like).

Serve Salad Niçoise as soon as you have assembled all the ingredients.

A boiled egg with strips of toast makes an ideal toddler breakfast.

Cheese and eggs

Cheese and eggs are protein-rich 'fast' foods which can play a useful part in children's diets. Cheese needs little or no preparation as a snack, and eggs take very little time to cook, though for babies and toddlers they must be cooked until both the yolk and white are solid.

For boiled eggs, bring the eggs to the boil in a pan of water and let them cook for 6–7 minutes. Serve with strips of toast. For successful poached eggs, you need really fresh eggs. Crack each egg carefully into a pan of simmering water and cook for 5–6 minutes. Remove with a slotted spoon to drain off the hot water and serve on a slice of lightly buttered toast.

Ingredients for Eggy bread (serves 4)

- *2 medium eggs*
- *2 tablespoons milk*
- *4 slices of bread*
- *a little olive oil*

Eggy bread

Most children like 'eggy bread' (also known as French toast) and you can vary the recipe sometimes by adding grated cheese to the egg mixture for a more substantial meal.

1. Beat the eggs and milk in a bowl.
2. Soak each slice of bread in the mixture.
3. Heat the oil in a non-stick frying pan and fry each slice for 2 minutes on each side.

Add a little black pepper to the beaten egg for extra flavour.

Ingredients for Cheese on toast (serves 1–2 toddlers)

- *55g (2oz) cheddar cheese (grated)*
- *1 slice of bread*

Cheese on toast

1. Heat the grill and toast the bread lightly on one side.
2. Turn the bread over and sprinkle with grated cheese.
3. Place back under the grill and toast until the cheese starts to bubble and brown. Remove and allow to cool.
4. Serve with cubes of cucumber and tomato.

Toddler omelette

Ingredients for
Toddler omelette
(serves 1 toddler)

• a little butter or oil
• 1 medium egg (beaten)
• grated cheese or pieces
  of ham (optional)

1. Melt the butter or heat the oil in a small frying pan.
   Pour in the egg and tilt the pan to spread it out.
2. Cook until the edges start to solidify. Using a wooden
   spatula, carefully turn the omelette over so it is cooked
   through on both sides.
3. Sprinkle on cheese or ham, fold omelette in half and serve.

Tasty tortilla

Ingredients for
Tasty tortilla (serves 4)

• 450g (1lb) potatoes (peeled
  and finely diced)
• 2 tablespoons olive oil
• 1 onion (finely chopped)
• 4 tablespoons cold water
• 4 eggs (beaten)
• sprig of fresh parsley
  (finely chopped)
• black pepper

Tortilla (or Spanish omelette) makes a filling breakfast, or
lunch with a salad. You can add other vegetables such as
peas, sweetcorn kernels or diced red pepper at step 4.

1. Heat a tablespoon of the oil in a large frying pan and fry
   the onions and potatoes for 5 minutes.
2. Add the water, cover the pan and cook on a low heat for
   15 minutes, or until the potatoes are soft.
3. Empty into a heat-proof bowl and stir in the eggs, pepper
   and parsley.
4. Heat the remaining oil in the frying pan and add the
   mixture. Cook on a low heat for 5–8 minutes.
5. To make sure both sides are cooked, place the pan under
   a grill, or flip the tortilla, and cook for a further 5 minutes.

You could serve tortilla
with home-made tomato
sauce (page 49).

Tasty tortilla and a
simple salad make a
well balanced meal.

Roasted vegetable couscous

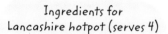

*Ingredients for
Roasted vegetable couscous
(serves 4)*

- *1 red pepper*
- *1 yellow pepper*
- *1 red onion (peeled)*
- *1 medium courgette*
- *1 aubergine*
- *12 cherry tomatoes (halved)*
- *1 tablespoon olive oil*
- *400g (14oz) couscous*
- *600ml (1 pint) boiling water*

1. Pre-heat the oven to 200°C, 400°F or gas mark 6.
2. Cut the peppers in half, remove the seeds and cores and cut the halves into pieces about 2.5cm (1in) square.
3. Cut the onion, courgette and aubergine into similar-sized pieces. Place them, with the peppers, in a roasting pan, drizzle with the oil and put in the oven for 15 minutes.
4. Add the tomatoes to the pan and cook for a further 15 minutes until the vegetables are beginning to brown.
5. Pour the boiling water over the couscous in another pan until fully absorbed. Serve with the vegetables on top and a spoonful of tomato sauce (see page 49) or passata.

Lancashire hotpot

*Ingredients for
Lancashire hotpot (serves 4)*

- *250g (9oz) lamb leg steak
  (diced into small cubes)*
- *350g (12oz) potatoes
  (peeled)*
- *100g (3 ½ oz) leeks (washed,
  trimmed and sliced)*
- *200g (7oz) carrots
  (peeled and sliced)*
- *400ml (²/₃ pint) low-salt
  vegetable stock*
- *sprig of thyme*

1. Pre-heat the oven to 180°C, 350°F or gas mark 4.
2. Cut two-thirds of the potatoes into small chunks and slice the remainder into thin slices.
3. Layer the meat, leeks, carrots and potato chunks in an oven-proof dish and add the sprig of thyme.
4. Layer the sliced potatoes on the top and pour over the stock. Cover and cook in the oven for 1 hour.
5. Turn up the oven to 200°C, 400°F or gas mark 6 and take the lid off the dish. Cook for a further 15 minutes.

*Remove the thyme sprig
before serving Lancashire
hotpot with chunky bread
for extra carbohydrate.*

Chicken and mash pie

Ingredients for
Chicken and mash pie
(4 toddler portions)

- 2 chicken breast fillets
- 1 small onion (peeled and quartered)
- 1 bayleaf
- 1 teaspoon parsley (chopped)
- 1 carrot (peeled and diced)
- 55g (2oz) frozen peas
- 55g (2oz) frozen sweetcorn
- 300g (10oz) potatoes (peeled and diced)
- 30g (1oz) butter
- 30g (1oz) plain flour
- 200ml (⅓ pint) milk

Safety point

You need to make sure all the recipes on these pages have cooled before you serve them to your toddler.

This can also be made with a mycoprotein vegetarian alternative for chicken, or with white fish fillets.

1. Cook the chicken in a pan of water with onion, bayleaf and carrot for 15 minutes or until the chicken is cooked.
2. At the same time boil the potatoes until they are soft.
3. Set the oven to 180°C, 350°F or gas mark 4.
4. Strain the chicken, carrot and onion and discard the bayleaf. Dice the chicken and onion.
5. Make a sauce by melting the butter and stirring in the flour. Remove pan from the heat and slowly add the milk. Return to heat and stir until thickened. Add the parsley.
6. In a casserole dish, mix together the sauce with the chicken and all the vegetables.
7. Mash the potatoes and spread over the chicken mixture.
8. Bake in the oven for 30 minutes until heated through and golden brown on top.

Older children may enjoy mashing the potatoes for this recipe.

Little lamb koftas

Ingredients for
Little lamb koftas (serves 4)

- 450g (1lb) lean minced lamb
- 1 small onion (peeled and finely chopped)
- 1 clove of garlic (peeled and finely chopped)
- 1 tablespoon fresh mint (chopped)
- 1 tablespoon fresh parsley (chopped)
- 1 teaspoon cumin powder

1. Put the onion, garlic and lamb in a large bowl and mix.
2. Stir in the parsley, mint and cumin. Leave the mixture in the refrigerator for 1 hour.
3. Divide the mixture into 12 balls and roll them with your fingers to make mini sausage shapes.
4. Grill for about 10 minutes, turning often until cooked thoroughly and starting to brown.
5. Serve with white rice, a tomato and cucumber salad and tomato sauce (see page 49), or a chilli sauce for adults.

Fish such as herring and mackerel are an important part of a healthy diet.

Getting more fish into the diet

All fish is a good source of protein and iodine, and oil-rich fish such as salmon, trout, sardines, herring, fresh tuna and mackerel are also a good source of Omega-3 fatty acids (which protect against heart disease) as well as iron and vitamins A and D. Nutritionists advise that everyone should try to eat two portions of fish a week, one of which should be an oil-rich fish. Tinned tuna does not contain enough fat to count as an oil-rich fish, but is a convenient form of fish to serve to toddlers. Salmon is versatile and a good way of getting more fish into your toddler's diet.

Pasta with smoked salmon

Many children like smoked salmon but be aware it is high in salt, so it's best to only serve it to toddlers occasionally and in small quantities.

Ingredients for
Pasta with smoked salmon
(for 2 adults and a toddler)
- 250g (9oz) pasta shapes of your choice
- 125g (4oz) smoked salmon cut into pieces
- 125g (4oz) full-fat fromage frais
- 1 teaspoon chopped parsley
- 125g (4oz) frozen peas

1. Cook the pasta in a pan of boiling water (following the timing on the packet, plus 1 minute). Add the peas a couple of minutes before the end.
2. Drain the pasta and peas and, while still hot, stir in the salmon, fromage frais and parsley.
3. Allow to stand for a few minutes until the fish has turned pale pink, then serve immediately.

Some children take longer than others to learn to eat pasta with a fork.

Toddler salmon teriyaki

*Ingredients for
Toddler salmon teriyaki
(serves 4)*

- 4 fillets of fresh salmon
- grated zest of half an orange
- juice of 1 orange
- 1 tablespoon runny honey
- 1 tablespoon low-sodium light soy or teriyaki sauce
- 1 tablespoon white wine vinegar or cider vinegar
- 1 clove of garlic (peeled and finely chopped)
- small piece of root ginger (peeled and grated)

You can use small salmon steaks or fillets for this recipe.

This works well with salmon but the same marinade can be used for chicken fillets and gives them a sticky, sweet and sour coating which many children like. Use low-salt soy or teriyaki sauce, if you can get it, and serve the fish or chicken with rice and a green vegetable or salad.

1. Put all the ingredients except the salmon into a bowl and mix well to make a marinade.
2. Put the salmon fillets into the marinade, cover and put in the refrigerator for at least 30 minutes.
3. Transfer the salmon onto a piece of foil, skin side down on the rack of a grill pan. Spoon the remaining marinade over the fish.
4. Grill the salmon for about 5 minutes on each side under a hot grill, spooning any marinade back over the fish when you turn it. (If you are using chicken fillets, grill for 6 to 8 minutes each side.)
5. Use a knife to check that the food is cooked through, and check carefully for any bones before serving.

Home-made fish fingers

*Ingredients for
Home-made fish fingers
(serves 4)*

- 3 slices of wholemeal bread (crusts removed)
- 2 tablespoons parsley (chopped)
- juice of a large lemon
- 225g (8oz) white fish such as hake, pollack or coley, or fresh tuna steak (all skinned and boned)

These fish fingers go very well with potato wedges (recipe on page 44) and some home-made tomato sauce (page 49). You could also use strips of skinless chicken in place of fish to make chicken goujons. Just increase the cooking time by 5 minutes.

1. Set the oven to 200°C, 400°F or gas mark 6.
2. In a blender or food processor, blitz the bread to make breadcrumbs, and then stir in the parsley.
3. Cut the fish into strips roughly 8 x 2cm (3 x 1in).
4. Put the lemon juice into a bowl and dip in the fish, then dunk it into the breadcrumbs making sure each strip is covered all over.
5. Place on a baking tray and cook in the oven for about 15 minutes, turning once halfway through.

Desserts

Desserts are often thought of as intrinsically unhealthy because of their high sugar content, but if you use them to get fruit and dairy products into young children's diets, and keep a firm eye on the amount of sugar you add, there's no reason that desserts can't play a part in a healthy diet. Keep any very sweet, rich desserts just for occasional treats, though.

Quick raspberry fool

*Ingredients for
Quick raspberry fool
(serves 4)*

- 175g (6oz) raspberries
- 30g (1oz) soft brown sugar
- 225g (8oz) fromage frais
- 1 teaspoon lemon juice

1. Keep a few of the raspberries back for decoration. Using a fork, crush the rest to a lumpy mush and then stir in the lemon juice and sugar.
2. Pour the fromage frais into a bowl and beat with a hand whisk until thickened.
3. Fold in the mashed raspberries and then spoon the fool into separate small bowls.

*Chill the raspberry
fool before decorating
and serving.*

Useful tip

*You could cook the
roasted vegetables on
page 56 at the same
time as baked apples.*

Baked apples

*Ingredients for
Baked apples*

- 1 large cooking apple
  per adult and half
  for each small child

For each apple you need:

- small handful of sultanas
- 1 teaspoon butter
- 1 teaspoon brown sugar

1. Set the oven to 200°C, 400°F or gas mark 6.
2. Wash the apples and remove the cores (using a corer or sharp knife) leaving a hole in the middle.
3. Score the skin around the widest part of each apple and place the apples in an oven-proof dish.
4. Mix together sultanas, sugar and butter and spoon the mixture into the holes of each apple. Press down firmly.
5. Bake for 20–30 minutes or until the apples are tender when pierced with a knife.

Home-made jelly

Ingredients for
Home-made jelly (serves 4)

- 450ml (³/4 pint) fruit juice
- sachet of powdered
  gelatine

Use any fruit juice for this recipe (orange works well). You can pour the jelly over fresh or canned fruit, but drain any juice from the can first, as this stops the jelly from setting.

1. Follow the packet instructions for making gelatine, using the fruit juice as your liquid.
2. Pour into bowls and allow to set in the refrigerator for a few hours before serving.

Toddler trifle

Ingredients for
Toddler trifle (serves 4)

- home-made jelly
  (recipe above)
- 1 banana (peeled and sliced)
- small punnet of raspberries,
  or strawberries (halved)

For the custard

- 300ml (¹/2 pint) milk
- 1 tablespoon cornflour
- 30g (1 oz) caster sugar
- 3 eggs (separated)
- a few drops of vanilla essence

This trifle uses fresh fruit but leaves out sugary trifle sponges. You can use ready-made custard and packet jelly to make it easier, but be aware this ups the sugar content.

1. Retaining a few berries for the top, place the fruit in the bottom of a glass bowl or in individual bowls. Pour on the jelly and leave to set.
2. Whisk the egg yolks, cornflour, sugar and vanilla essence together in a pan.
3. Heat the milk in another pan until boiling and stir into the egg mixture. Return to the heat and stir until thick.
4. Remove from the heat and allow to cool, then pour over the set jelly. Chill and decorate before serving.

These trifles have been decorated with fromage frais, raspberries and some crushed ginger biscuits.

Sultana scones
make a good
toddler snack any
time of the day.

Sultana scones

Scones make a useful carbohydrate-rich snack at times of
flagging energy, and don't contain any added sugar.
A tablespoon of sultanas added to the flour helps to
sweeten these scones and also counts towards fruit
servings for the day. Wholemeal flour produces good
scones, as does a mixture of half white and half wholemeal
flour. This makes 12 scones with a 6cm (2½in) cutter or
24 mini-scones with a 4cm (1½in) cutter.

Ingredients for Sultana scones

- 225g (8oz) self-raising flour
- 55g (2oz) butter
- 150ml (¹/₄ pint) full-fat milk
- 1 tablespoon sultanas

1. Pre-heat the oven to 220°C, 425°F or gas mark 7.
2. Rub the butter into the flour to make fine breadcrumbs.
3. Add the milk a little at a time, stirring with a knife.
4. Flour your hands and gently knead the mixture into a
   ball. Add a little more milk if it is too dry and crumbly.
5. Sprinkle some flour onto a work surface and roll out the
   dough until it is about 2cm (¾in) thick.
6. Using a round cookie cutter, cut out scones and place
   them on a greased baking tray.
7. Bake the scones near the top of the oven for 12–15
   minutes until golden brown.

You could serve scones cut
in half with cream cheese,
fromage frais or unsalted
butter spread on top.

Plain or fruity pancakes

Pancakes are quick to prepare (especially if you make the batter in advance), are low in fat and salt, and you can control how much sugar goes onto them. You could try using half wholemeal and half white flour.

1. Place the flour in a bowl and make a well in the middle.
2. Add the egg and pour in the milk gradually, mixing to form a smooth batter.
3. Leave to stand for at least half an hour before using.
4. Melt a knob of butter in a frying pan and pour in a ladleful of batter. When the sides begin to set, shake the pancake and flip it over with a spatula.
5. Cook for 1 minute and serve.

To make apple pancakes, peel, core and thinly slice an eating apple and fry in a tiny bit of butter in the pancake pan until soft. Ladle the batter over the apple and cook. You can cook pears, plums or berries in the same way.

Ingredients for Plain pancakes (serves 4)

- 125g (4oz) plain flour (sifted)
- 1 large egg (beaten)
- 300ml (¹/₂ pint) milk
- knob of butter

You can add flavourings to plain pancakes such as a drizzle of maple syrup or a little sugar and lemon juice.

Fruit milk shakes and smoothies

Home-made milk shakes and smoothies are a useful way to get extra fruit into your child's diet and keep up their dairy intake. Just put all the ingredients in a blender, whiz until blended and frothy and serve in a beaker with a straw. You could experiment using half yogurt or fromage frais and half milk for milk shakes. As well as fresh fruit, try frozen berries, or fruit canned in juice – canned mango works especially well.

Fresh milk shakes and smoothies make healthy treats to offer toddlers.

Ingredients for Mango smoothie

- 1 small banana (peeled and broken into chunks)
- 150ml (¹/₄ pint) apple juice (chilled)
- half a ripe fresh, or canned, mango (roughly cubed)

Ingredients for Strawberry milk shake

- 10 fresh strawberries (washed and hulled)
- 150ml (¹/₃ pint) semi-skimmed milk
- little pot of strawberry fromage frais

Preventing fussy eating

Many toddlers insist on eating the same foods over and over again and tend to reject anything new. Having cereal for breakfast, a sandwich for lunch and pasta in the evening provides a familiar and comforting routine, and getting them to eat a more varied diet can be a challenge. It's important, however, to keep offering new foods to toddlers in as calm a way as possible, even though they may refuse them time and time again. Children often become more adventurous when out of a familiar environment, so holidays, meals out or visits to friends are good times to introduce new foods.

Happy mealtimes

• Make sure meals are sociable, friendly occasions.

• Let children play with their food before they eat it.

• Put a new food on the table or plate along with everything else. Don't draw attention to it.

• Keep portions small and don't insist children eat everything on their plate.

• Let children feed themselves, even if this takes longer than you would like.

• Let toddlers sample food from your plate if they want.

• Avoid getting angry if your child refuses to eat something.

• Don't give too many drinks or snacks in between meals.

• Only keep foods you want your child to eat in the house.

• Be a good role model – try to eat well yourself.

Meals with friends are good times to offer new foods.

Asserting independence

Fussy eating may have less to do with the actual food than your toddler testing the limits of your authority. When they realize that you can't *make* them eat and drink, meals offer an opportunity to assert some control over their lives. This is why putting pressure on toddlers to eat something often results in their refusal to do so. They realize that they get attention just by saying 'no'. For this reason, remember to praise your child when they do eat, and just remove food that they don't want without comment and without showing that you are worried, upset or angry.

Enough is enough

The average one to two year-old needs around 1000 calories a day – but small children's food intake and appetites fluctuate and can vary greatly from day to day. It is better not to compare what your child eats with what other children eat, as they are all different. It is important not to give toddlers large portions that you will then try to persuade them to eat. Start with a small portion (one to two tablespoons of a main dish for example) and offer a second helping if your child is still hungry. Children are unlikely to overeat if they are offered a variety of healthy foods at meal and snack times. If your toddler has a very small appetite at meals, make sure they are not having snacks or drinks beforehand which blunt their appetite.

Your child is telling you they have had enough when:

• They hold food in their mouth without swallowing it.

• They keep pushing the food or the spoon away when you are feeding them.

• They keep turning their head away from the food.

• They cry or scream, spit the food out, gag or vomit.

'Don't like it...'

There will be foods that children just don't like because of their texture, colour or taste. A food could remind them of something they've had before which they didn't like, or maybe the last time coincided with them not feeling well. Whatever the reason, forcing them to eat something can be counter-productive. If you avoid putting pressure on a child so they feel it is safe to say 'no' to certain foods, they're more likely to remain open to trying other new foods.

Useful tip

It's not a good idea to use food as a reward or bribe. If you offer ice cream as a reward for eating carrots, it coveys the message that ice cream is desirable and carrots are not.

While it is difficult not to worry about what your child eats, studies show that children are generally good at eating a balanced diet over time and do not choose to starve themselves. If you are really worried about your child's diet and think it could be affecting their health, talk to your health visitor or doctor.

Don't put pressure on toddlers to eat when they are just not interested.

Healthy snacks

Toddler snack ideas

- cut up cucumber, carrots and tomatoes
- chunks of fruit, such as banana and apple
- seedless grapes (cut in half) and small pieces of cheese
- rice cakes (salt-free)
- fingers of wholemeal bread or toast
- breadsticks (salt-free)
- small sandwiches with savoury fillings
- plain popcorn
- natural yogurt

Healthy drinks

These are suitable drinks for children over 12 months and under five years:

- full-fat milk (children who eat well can have semi-skimmed as their main drink from the age of two)
- still water
- diluted fruit juice with meals
- a small quantity of fruit smoothie or home-made milk shake (with meals)

Plain popcorn is a very good snack for toddlers.

Little children's stomachs are too small to take in enough food to last until the next meal, so snacks are a vital part of a toddler's diet. Having a supply of snacks on hand also makes your life easier, as they help keep children in a happy mood. It's important that snacks are varied and nutrient-dense, so use a range of bread-based snacks with savoury fillings or dips, or fresh fruit with yogurt or rice pudding. Dried fruit can stick to teeth and contribute to dental decay, so is better only served with meals. Attractive packaging often appeals to toddlers, so try serving snacks in pretty paper bags, clean yogurt pots or small bowls.

Toddlers need healthy snacks between meals.

Are sweets allowed?

For toddlers under two, it may be possible to delay the consumption of sweets until they are older (especially if they are the oldest child). In reality, however, children are likely to be exposed to sweets as they get older and the best bet can be to allow some (so they don't become a forbidden fruit) but control when and what they eat. If children do have sweets, the best time is after a meal, and you could save them for special occasions. Avoid any sweets with artificial colours, those which are chewy or stick to teeth, and those which might cause choking or could get stuck in an ear or nose. A few chocolate buttons as an occasional treat are unlikely to upset the balance of your child's diet.

Fun with food

Getting children involved in choosing and preparing what they are going to eat is a great way to help them enjoy food and be interested in healthy eating. Even from a very young age, children can participate in shopping and food preparation, and can start learning about where food comes from. This section also has ideas for simple and healthy party foods and treats.

At a glance

Taking your child shopping and involving them in choosing what to eat

How to make your kitchen a safe place for children

Ideas for kitchen activities to do with babies and toddlers

Preparing for, and enjoying, children's parties

Going shopping

Food shopping can be a significant learning experience for toddlers, and they are more likely to behave well in shops and be interested in what they eat at home if you can involve them in some way in choosing and buying food. Whether you go to a supermarket, farm shop or fishmonger, try to use the opportunity to chat with your child about what they can see; let them taste, touch and choose some items when possible, and talk to them about where different kinds of food come from.

Involving children

Children often respond well to being given choices about what they eat:

• Let your child decide whether to buy red or green apples and help them to put them into a bag.

• They could choose a new vegetable to try, and help you wash it when you get home.

• If you go to a market which offers little tasters, let your child try a couple to see which they like best.

Watching what you buy

Some pre-prepared foods, and foods that have been made to have a longer shelf-life or to be transported long distances, may contain ingredients you would not use when cooking at home. Everyone will use some processed foods in their diets such as breakfast cereals, cheese, bread or milk, but it can be useful to look carefully at labels to avoid processed foods that appear to contain a lot of added salt, sugar or artificial sweeteners (see page 15 for how to read a label). Foods prepared for the adult market are unlikely to be suitable for toddlers, especially things such as savoury snacks, instant drink powders, ready-made sauces and foods which are made with hydrogenated fats, such as many cakes, biscuits and pastries.

Children start to develop an understanding of food if you talk to them about where it comes from and they help you choose it.

Where to buy food

Supermarkets have made food shopping with small children easier in some respects (especially if you shop online) but going to a butcher's, greengrocer's or baker's often provides a richer experience for them. The shop staff are usually geared towards customers in a way that supermarket staff may not be, and they may be able to tell you more about their produce and where it comes from. Individual shops or stalls also highlight the fact that food comes from several sources and not just from one centralized location. Local farmers' markets and street markets can also help open children's eyes to the variety of food available.

Farm shopping

• 'Pick your own' fruit farms are fun for toddlers. Strawberries are especially easy for them to pick and make great smoothies (see page 63 for recipe).

• Child-friendly 'open' farms and farm parks let children meet animals and help them learn about where food comes from.

• Farm shops and farmers' markets specialize in local produce and usually encourage plenty of browsing and tasting.

A visit to a farm helps children find out about where food comes from.

Resisting 'pester power'

Even little children are influenced by advertising and learn to recognize television characters on packaging and the branding for fast food outlets, cereals, soft drinks, sweets and savoury snacks. Sadly, the diet advertised to children usually contrasts greatly with the one recommended by dieticians, so you need to resist pressure to buy the brands when shopping. You can often distract toddlers by getting them to look for foods that you do want to buy and by talking about the tasty things you are going to make. Keep shopping trips brisk and chatty and most toddlers won't keep demanding a food once it is out of their view.

Did you know?

Studies have shown that the more food advertisements children of school-age see, the more unhealthy snacks and calories they actually consume.

Kitchen safety

Little children usually love 'helping' in the kitchen, and involving them in food preparation, when you can, is one way to encourage an interest in the food they eat. However, the kitchen is the most dangerous room in the home and as under-threes can't be expected to understand or remember safety advice, it's up to you to supervise them very carefully at all times, and make your kitchen as safe as possible before you let them do any 'cooking'. Keeping things clean in the kitchen (and bathroom) is important for everyone's health and safety. Highchair trays, kitchen floors and rubbish bins need particular attention.

Door dangers

If cupboards are at floor level, make sure children can't reach anything in them that may be poisonous, breakable or dangerous. Child locks are the best option as toddlers usually can't resist rummaging in cupboards. If you can, leave one unsecured cupboard filled with plastic kitchen toys, wooden spoons and light saucepans as a safe distraction. You can add and remove objects to keep toddlers interested.

Make sure refrigerator doors are secured so toddlers can't pull them open and have items fall on their head, or affect the temperature of the food. (Food has to be kept at below 5°C or 41°F to prevent bacterial growth.) Remove magnets from doors so children can't put them in their mouths.

A few child-friendly cooking implements and toys can help your toddler to feel involved.

Hot things

Hot liquids are a constant source of danger to young children in the home as they can create a burn in a few seconds. Do not carry babies or toddlers while holding a hot drink, teapot, kettle or coffee jug and always place hot liquids well out of their reach. Deep-fat fryers should be used with great care (and deep-fat fried foods should only be eaten occasionally) as hot fat can cause serious burns. Old-fashioned chip pans should not be used at all. To help keep small children away from the cooker, mark a boundary at least 50cm (20in) away from it using coloured tape on the floor. Teach your child not to cross this line (but remember this is no substitute for adult supervision).

Rubbish bins

Make sure that anything you put in rubbish, recycling or kitchen compost bins stays out of the reach of little hands. Broken glass, can lids, bleach leaking from a bottle or raw egg from egg shells are all dangerous hazards for small children. Bins should be kept behind a closed door secured with a child lock. Empty and clean out bins regularly with hot soapy water. This will help control bugs and bacteria as well as protecting your child.

Did you know?

Nearly two-thirds of domestic fires start because of something to do with cooking, and most of these start when people are distracted or leave things unattended.

Keep bins clean and out of the reach of babies and toddlers.

A travel cot or playpen can keep your child out of harm's way when you are dealing with rubbish and hot things.

In the kitchen together

You have bought the ingredients and made sure your kitchen is safe, but before you let your child 'do some cooking', there are a few more things to consider, such as mess control, basic hygiene and considering what they can actually do. The tips on the left will help you prepare as far as you can, and there are some ideas below for helping involve children at different ages and stages:

At 6 months your baby will enjoy being in the kitchen with you. Let them sit in their highchair and play with some safe plastic crockery and wooden utensils.

By 12 months many babies will be able to use a spoon. Whether they bang it on a pan or help stir cake mix, this gets them used to handling implements.

By 14 months children may have discovered the fun of emptying containers. Provide a few different-sized boxes and fill them with a little cereal or dried pasta for children to pour into plastic bowls. They will also enjoy filling and emptying cups of water.

At 18 months many children begin to be able to sort by colour and shape. Cut up red, green and yellow peppers, carrots, tomatoes and cucumber and help your child to sort them into different bowls.

Two and three-year olds often enjoy mixing, stirring, rolling and decorating. You could let them sprinkle on the cheese to make cheese on toast (page 54) or pizzas (page 51), put the fruit in the blender to make smoothies (page 63) and help mix the ingredients to make scones (page 62) or help make the pastry and decorate these little fruit tarts.

Ready to cook

• Dress your child in a waterproof apron or overalls. Roll up long sleeves.

• Tie back long hair and help make sure everyone washes their hands thoroughly and and dries them carefully.

• Make sure children can reach a work surface safely by standing on a sturdy stool, box or chair, or let them kneel on a chair at a table.

A few mini-baking utensils may keep your child occupied.

A play cooker can be fun for toddlers (a big box will do) and may satisfy their desire to do some cooking, for a while.

Little fruit tarts

Ingredients for
Little fruit tarts
(makes 12)

For the shortcrust pastry:

- 125g (4oz) plain white flour
- 55g (2oz) butter
- 2 tablespoons cold water

For the custard:

- 300ml (1/2 pint) milk
- 1 teaspoon cornflour
- a few drops of vanilla essence
- 3 egg yolks
- 1 tablespoon caster sugar

For the filling:

- Soft fruit such as raspberries,
  strawberries and kiwi fruit
  (cut into small pieces)

You could use ready-made pastry and custard for this recipe, but part of the fun for a toddler is seeing the dough come together. You need two rolling pins (a mini-one for your child) a twelve-cup baking tray and a large cookie cutter.

1. Let your child help you rub the butter into the flour in a bowl and sprinkle on the water to make pastry. Knead for a few seconds and put in a plastic bag in the refrigerator for 30 minutes.
2. Set the oven to 200°C, 400°F or gas mark 6.
3. Pour the milk into a pan with the vanilla essence and heat until almost boiling. Whisk the egg yolks, cornflour and sugar together and stir in the hot milk.
4. Return to the pan and heat for 10–20 minutes until thick. Remove from the heat and stir occasionally until cool to prevent a skin forming.
5. Give your child a small piece of the pastry and a rolling pin to play with while you roll out the rest on a floured worktop. Let them help you cut out 8 circles. Knead the remaining dough and roll again for the other 4 circles.
6. Place the pastry circles in the baking tray and prick with a fork. Bake in the oven for 10 minutes.
7. When cooked and cooled, spoon in a teaspoon of the custard and let your child drop on the fruit.

Let your child use a pastry brush to glaze the tarts with warmed, runny jam (but make sure it's not too hot).

Food for parties

At a party, babies and toddlers are usually much more interested in playing with giftwrap, balloons and the people around them than in the contents of the sandwiches and the standard of cake decoration. If you are preparing party food, it's a good idea to keep things simple so you can enjoy the special day too. Make sure there are enough adults to help supervise children eating, and clear away the leftovers promptly. Avoid lots of food and drink with sugar in them – a few treats, such as a cake and some home-made fizzy drinks (see below) are fine, but make sure there are healthy, savoury things on offer too. Here are some ideas:

- pizza in small squares (page 50)
- little sandwiches or rolls
- small lumps of cheese
- potato wedges (page 44)
- plain popcorn
- cherry tomatoes (halved)
- carrot sticks
- bread sticks

- hummus (for dipping)
- raisins and sultanas
- seedless grapes (halved)
- small chunks of banana
- satsuma segments
- toddler trifle (page 61)
- jelly (page 61) and ice-cream
- little fruit tarts (page 73)

Party food tips

- Organize a party near a normal mealtime, trying to avoid nap times.

- Check if any guests have allergies or special diets beforehand.

- Serve the food early on to avoid tired, hungry babies and toddlers.

- Bring out the savoury food before the sweet stuff.

- Keep drinks available at all times.

Useful tip

Don't worry if party guests don't eat much. Babies and toddlers often lose their appetites when they are excited.

For toddlers, presents and playing are usually more important than the party food.

Party drinks

At a party, children can enjoy special drinks and as long as these are drunk with food it doesn't matter if they contain sugar or are fruit based (but avoid drinks which contain artificial sweeteners). You could try fresh fruit juice diluted with fizzy water, a milk shake or smoothie (see page 63) or fizzy water with ice cubes made from fresh fruit juice.

Keep party food and drinks simple.

Special diets and activity

In this section there's advice on how to make sure vegetarian diets include all the nutrients young children need. There is also information about food allergies and intolerances, and how to make sure children stay a healthy weight for their height and get plenty of exercise.

At a glance

Making sure a vegetarian diet is well balanced and provides all the essential nutrients children need

What to do if you think your child has a food allergy and how this may affect their overall diet

How to help children stay a healthy weight, and making sure that they stay active

Vegetarian and vegan diets

Vegetarians avoid eating meat and fish and may also exclude foods that contain gelatine or animal rennet from their diet. Vegetarians do eat dairy products and eggs which are useful sources of many nutrients. It is perfectly possible for children to get all the nutrients they need from a vegetarian diet, but you do need to take a little more care to ensure you serve a wide variety of foods, especially sources of iron (see left). It's also especially important that vegetarian children have vitamin drops (see page 86).

Vegans avoid all animal products so rely entirely on plant sources for their nutrients. A vegan diet is not recommended for children under five, but if you do want your child to be a vegan, you should seek advice from a health professional on how to do this safely. For sources of help, visit the Usborne Quicklinks Website (see page 91).

First vegetarian foods

Between six and twelve months, babies need 700 to 1000 calories a day, but can't eat large quantities. As a general rule, avoid vegetarian foods which are bulky or watery and aim to serve concentrated energy foods, such as lentils with vegetable oil or avocado, cheese or smooth nut butters. Vitamin C aids the absorption of iron from plant food, so it helps to serve sources of iron and vitamin C together (spinach and apple purée for example). Vitamin C is found in fresh, frozen or juiced fruit and vegetables.

Vegetarian sources of important nutrients

Iron: wholegrain and fortified cereals, dark green vegetables, green beans, peas, dried fruit, nuts, eggs, pulses such as lentils and beans, and soya products.

Protein: nuts, seeds, eggs, milk, beans and pulses contain high levels. Also in grains and cereals such as wheat, rice, sweetcorn and oats.

Calcium: tofu, cheese, yogurt, green vegetables, ground seeds and nuts. Also in cow's and fortified soya milk (but only to be used in the later stages of weaning).

Zinc: breakfast cereals, nuts, eggs, milk, cheese, beans and lentils, sesame seeds.

B vitamins: fortified breakfast cereals, yeast extract, nuts, eggs, cheese and wholemeal bread are all good sources.

Like all children, vegetarian children need to spend time outside each day, as sunlight provides vitamin D. (But don't put babies in full sun.)

Vegetarian babies need small, frequent meals and concentrated energy foods.

A vegetarian diet should be varied and low in sugar and salt.

Example diet from 12 months

Breakfast: Porridge with banana slices, or boiled egg with toast fingers and halved cherry tomatoes.

Mid-morning: Milk drink, bread sticks and cucumber with hummus, or yogurt and berries.

Lunch: Pasta with fresh pesto and green beans, or mushroom omelette with sweetcorn. Rice pudding with raisins, or fruity pancakes.

Mid-afternoon: Milk drink and apple chunks.

Early evening: Egg and cress sandwiches, carrot sticks or home-made baked beans with pitta bread fingers. Sultana scones and raspberries, or fruit salad. Milk drink before bed.

Vegetarian foods to avoid

There are many ready-made vegetarian foods on the market, but they're mostly designed for adults and are not suitable for young children because of their high salt content. Check labels on foods such as vegetarian burgers and sausages and avoid any which contain more than 1.25g (0.5g sodium) per 100g. Toddlers should not have more than 2g of salt (0.8g sodium) a day. Some vegetarian foods may also be high in fibre and very bulky and may make a child feel full before they have eaten all the nutrients they need. Simple, home-made vegetarian meals such as those suggested on this page are usually a better option.

Recipes to try

6 to 8 months (p.24 – 34):

- One-vegetable purée
- Butter bean casserole
- Lentils with spinach
- Cheesy leeks and potato
- Apricot semolina

9 to 11 months (p.38 – 44):

- Fruity porridge
- Scrambled eggs
- Pea and parmesan risotto
- Rice and red lentils
- Red pepper and tomato rice
- Pasta and fresh pesto
- Little cheesy baked potato
- Home-made baked beans
- Potato wedges

From one year (p.48 – 66):

- Macaroni cheese
- Cheat's pizza
- Bean salad
- Tasty tortilla
- Roasted vegetable couscous
- Fruity pancakes
- Sultana scones

Safety point

Remember that whole nuts and seeds must not be given to under-fives. Ground nuts such as smooth peanut butter can be given (unless there are allergies in the family).

Food allergy and intolerance

Experts use the term 'food hypersensitivity' to describe unpleasant reactions to food. These may be caused by a food allergy or a food intolerance. While many parents worry that their child may have a sensitivity to a type of food, only about one baby in twelve is likely to react to food, and most grow out of these reactions by the time they are three. Only about two per cent of children remain allergic to one or more foods as they grow older. Children most at risk are those who have parents or brothers and sisters with a food allergy, asthma, eczema or hay fever.

Keep an eye on your baby after introducing a new food to check for any signs of a reaction.

Safety point

Seek urgent medical help if a baby has any kind of swelling in the mouth or throat area or has difficulty breathing.

Rapid symptoms of an allergic response

• Wheezing
• Swelling of lips, tongue and face and difficulty breathing
• Rashes
• Itching and redness
• Vomiting

Foods most likely to cause these are peanuts, tree nuts (such as almonds, cashews, hazelnuts, walnuts and Brazil nuts), fish, eggs, shellfish and sesame seeds. Milk, wheat and soya cause severe reactions more rarely.

Less rapid symptoms

• eczema
• diarrhoea
• constipation
• vomiting
  (a few hours after a meal)
• abdominal pain
• bloating, wind
• colic, wheezing

These symptoms may appear a few hours after eating and are most likely to be caused by milk, wheat or soya. They are caused more rarely by tree nuts, peanuts, fish, shellfish, sesame seeds or eggs.

Food allergy

A food allergy is a reaction to a food – most often a protein – and the reaction involves the body's immune system. The response may be rapid and severe or slower and less severe (see left), depending on how the immune system reacts. If your child has any such reactions to a food, do not give them the food again without seeking medical advice from your doctor or from a registered dietician. Make sure that everyone who takes care of your child understands the importance of avoiding any foods which may trigger this kind of reaction. If your child attends a nursery, explain your child's allergy and check that an allergy plan is in place.

Allergy to milk

If you have a history of allergies in your family, then exclusively breast-feeding your baby is the best way to protect them from an allergic reaction in the first six months. Formula milk contains cow's milk protein and can cause a serious reaction in some babies. If your baby appears to have a reaction to formula milk, it is important to seek advice from a doctor or registered dietician. They may recommend a hydrolysed formula or soya formula. Don't change to a soya or other non-dairy formula milk without talking to a medical professional first, as such products can also cause allergies. Remember that cow's, goat's or sheep's milk is not suitable for babies under 12 months.

Avoiding reactions

• *Breast-feeding until six months helps to reduce the chance of your baby developing allergies.*

• *Introduce new foods one by one and watch for signs of a reaction.*

• *Consider using organic produce to avoid residues which occasionally cause allergic reactions.*

• *Check labels for ingredients and additives (see page 13) you may want to avoid.*

Food intolerance

If a child has a food intolerance, they may have an unpleasant reaction to a food but this doesn't involve their immune system. The symptoms can appear quickly but are rarely life-threatening. Foods which commonly cause this kind of reaction are listed on the right, but a child could be intolerant to any food or drink. The best advice if your baby shows a food intolerance is to omit the food from their diet for a few weeks and then try it again. If there is a further reaction then avoid this food until your baby is a little older, then try again.

Being unable to eat certain foods is unlikely to harm a child's health, but you should get advice before excluding whole food groups from a child's diet.

The most common food intolerances are to:

• *milk and cheese*
• *citrus fruits*
• *strawberries*
• *bananas*
• *avocados*
• *chocolate*
• *fish*
• *yeast extract*

Symptoms of a food intolerance may occur quickly or a few hours after eating and include:

• *eczema, rashes*
• *vomiting*
• *diarrhoea*
• *stomach cramps*

Healthy weight reminders

• When weaning, introduce a variety of savoury foods and fruit purées.

• Don't push your baby into finishing food if they have shown they have had enough.

• Ensure children have at least five tastes of different fruits and vegetables each day.

• Avoid giving drinks other than water or milk between meals. Serve diluted juice at mealtimes only.

• Don't use sweet foods as a bribe or reward or for comfort.

• Avoid snacks that are high in fat, salt or sugar.

Healthy weight gain

Most babies double their birth weight by four or five months and triple it by their first birthday. However, unless you, your health visitor or doctor have particular worries about your baby's growth and development, there is no need to have their weight checked very frequently. As long as they are feeding well, have several nappy changes a day and seem bright and alert for some of each day, they are likely to be doing well. It's unlikely that your baby will gain too much weight if you breast-feed on demand or provide exactly the amount of formula milk suggested and wean them onto a wide variety of healthy foods (as described in this book).

The right amount of milk

Breast-fed babies have been shown in some studies to be less likely to be overweight in later life. It is thought this is because they are able to regulate their energy intake better than formula-fed babies. If you bottle-feed, it's important that you always make up the formula milk carefully (see page 21). Adding even a little extra powder at each feed can lead to your baby having more calories than they need.

When they start on solids, breast-fed babies automatically reduce the quantity of milk they consume. Remember that bottle-fed babies might also not want to finish their bottle when you start weaning them.

Urging a baby to finish a bottle as well as their food, might mean they consume more than they need.

Healthy, happy toddlers

Many toddlers appear chubby at the start of their second year, but will soon start to put on weight less rapidly as they become more mobile and active. If you are worried about your child's weight, consult your health visitor or doctor. You should never put a child under five years of age on a diet, or give them diet foods (such as low-fat or artificially sweetened foods). If their weight gain is too rapid, the aim should be to slow it down as they grow, not for the child to lose weight. To ensure young children stay a healthy weight, it is important to balance healthy eating with plenty of activity. There are ideas on how to keep children active on pages 82 and 83.

Make sure that watching television doesn't become associated with snacking on high-fat, high-salt or high-sugar junk food.

Regular, healthy snacks are an important part of a healthy diet for little children.

Sweet things

Most children love sweet things and the occasional treat won't hurt, but aim to keep sugary foods for mealtimes. To add sweetness to dishes, you could use:

- dessert apple purée
- mashed banana
- puréed apricots
- chopped up dried fruit such as dates
- strawberries, raspberries or blueberries

For sweet treats, offer:

- fruit purée ice lollies
- fruit jelly
- fruit kebabs
- frozen bananas

Comfort food

Sweets and biscuits are often given to little children to soothe them when they are upset, distract them when they have hurt themselves or occupy them when they are bored. They learn to associate these foods with providing comfort and this may continue into adulthood. It's important to find other ways to help a child get over unpleasant feelings and discomfort – distraction with a special toy, a cuddle, a song, some soothing words, or just drawing their attention to something else may work.

Baby moves

Lay your baby on their front
to encourage them to lift
their head to see what's
happening around them.

Put your baby on their back,
with a toy to their side, to
encourage them to roll over.

When they can hold their
head up, try a door bouncer.
Only use for ten to 20 minutes
at a time as it's very tiring.

Keeping them active

It is natural for babies to wriggle and move their bodies
and, as they grow, most want to become more active,
learning to roll over, sit up, crawl and then walk before
gradually acquiring the skills they need to kick a ball or ride
a tricycle. If your baby isn't crawling yet, you can still
encourage them to move in the ways shown on the left.

From the time your baby is sitting up, at around six
months, they can often hold a ball and roll or throw it –
although usually at this age they want to hold onto it for
themselves. In time, however, they will enjoy throwing the
ball to you and getting it back. A good way to start is by
rolling it to one another while sitting on the floor.

Older babies who can crawl or walk will naturally become
more and more active, burning up energy as they develop
their new skills. When your child starts to walk, make time
for regular little strolls along the road or around a park,
letting them hold their buggy or your hand for some of the
way. It may take longer, but they can't practise their new-
found skill if they are strapped in the buggy all the time.

*From about four months, babies learn
to raise their heads when lying on their
tummies — but it's very hard work.*

Useful tip

Many swimming pools have
parent and baby swim sessions.
For advice on going to the
pool with your child, visit the
Usborne Quicklinks Website
(see page 91).

Toddler fun

Toddlers usually love a trip to a playground to try out the swings and slides. Little children also enjoy chasing games, trying to kick and throw large soft balls, going swimming, exploring soft play areas and rolling around in ball pits. Getting into the habit of walking, rather than driving (when you can) benefits you both. Dancing and doing action rhymes also gets everyone moving and having fun. You could put on some favourite music and show toddlers some moves to copy. Get them to touch their toes, swing their arms around, do some hand movements or just jump about.

Blow some bubbles for your toddler to chase and burst.

Turn off the television

Everyone needs time for relaxation, but the television has become too big a part of many children's lives from an early age, and when they are watching television they are not being active. Until a child is two, it's important to limit television time very strictly (or not introduce it at all) and only ever let toddlers watch programmes specifically designed for their age group. You may want to put on a favourite DVD for them while you are cooking a meal, or watch a suitable programme together and talk about what you see. Childcare experts recommend that no child of any age is in front of any screen for more than two hours a day.

Activity checklist

• Tickle your baby — wriggling and giggling will give them a good work-out.

• Take your baby or toddler swimming as often as you can.

• Let your child walk beside you holding their buggy.

• Use local playgrounds and parks and have fun chasing your toddler.

• Supply 'active' toys, such as balls, prams and trucks to push and scooters and trikes.

• Do some action rhymes and songs. Visit the Usborne Quicklinks Website (see page 91) for ideas.

• Put a strict limit on the amount of television your child watches.

Useful information

In this final section of the book, you will find a glossary of terms to do with food and nutrition, charts which bring together some of the nutritional information in the book, a guide to weights and measures and some advice on what to do if your child starts choking. There is also some information about websites to visit where you can find out more about healthy eating for babies and toddlers.

At a glance

A glossary of the food and nutrition
terms used in the book

A chart showing important minerals and vitamins,
what they do, and their main sources

A feeding chart which shows what your child can
and can't eat at different ages and stages

Metric and imperial conversion tables for quantities
in recipes, and a table of oven temperatures

What to do if a baby or toddler starts choking

Useful websites to visit

Glossary

Allergy: a reaction to a food component (usually a protein) that triggers a response from the body's immune system. If a child has a serious reaction to a food, seek advice from your doctor.

Amino acids: substances used by the body to make proteins. Eight amino acids are termed 'essential' because they can't be made by the body and must be obtained from food.

Antioxidants: substances such as vitamin C or vitamin E that counteract the damaging effects of oxidation on the body. Antioxidants help to protect cell walls from damage caused by free radicals which are produced during the oxidation process.

Calcium: an essential mineral found in dairy products, green leafy vegetables, soya beans, nuts and bread. Calcium helps to build strong bones and teeth as well as helping blood clotting and functioning of nerves and muscles.

Carbohydrates: sugars, starches and fibre.

Colours: anything added to food to change its colour. Some colours are natural, others are artificial.

Fibre: a substance found in cereal foods and fruit and vegetables that is not fully broken down in the body and aids digestion and bowel function.

Folic acid: (also called folates) a B vitamin essential for healthy red blood cells and cell growth. Women planning a pregnancy are advised to take 400 micrograms of folic acid a day during the period of conception and up to the 12th week of pregnancy to reduce the risk of a baby with a neural tube defect such as spina bifida.

Formula milk: cow's milk which has been modified to make it suitable for babies to drink.

GM foods: foods made from genetically modified plants and animals which have had their DNA altered through genetic engineering.

Immune system: the way our bodies protect themselves against diseases.

Iodine: an element found in sea fish, shellfish, cereals and grains. It helps keep the cells in our bodies healthy.

Intolerance: a reaction to a food. Intolerances don't involve the body's immune system and are rarely life-threatening.

Iron: an essential mineral. Good sources of iron include liver, meat, beans, nuts, dried fruit, whole grains, fortified breakfast cereals and most dark green leafy vegetables.

Nutrients: foods or chemicals that living things need in order to grow and live.

Organic food: food that has been produced with restricted use of artificial fertilizers, pesticides and additives, no genetically modified ingredients, and an emphasis on animal welfare.

Pasteurization: a process of heating drinks (such as milk) in order to destroy harmful micro-organisms such as bacteria.

Protein: a substance needed for growth. Babies and toddlers need a greater proportion of it in their diet than adults.

Trans-fats: fats which have been treated with hydrogen to make them last longer. Many experts believe trans-fats increase cholesterol and can contribute to heart disease and other illnesses.

Vitamins and minerals

Vitamins and minerals are essential for good health and most have to come from food. Breast or formula milk provides all the vitamins and minerals a baby needs up to six months and for much of their first year. Once your child is fully weaned, the best way to ensure they get the full range is to provide a varied and balanced diet with foods from all the food groups, including plenty of fruit and vegetables. The chart on these pages shows some important minerals and vitamins and their main sources.

Safety point

Don't give any vitamin, mineral, food or herbal supplement to children, except on the advice of a qualified medical practitioner. Many of these products can be harmful to children.

Vitamin supplements

It is recommended that babies who are breast-fed have vitamin drops containing vitamins A, C and D from six months of age. Some parents may be advised to start their babies on vitamin drops earlier if they are at risk of vitamin D deficiency. Formula-fed babies should have extra vitamins once they drink less than 500mls (17 fl oz) of milk a day or when they go onto cow's milk as their main drink. Your doctor or health visitor can advise you on this.

Mineral	What does it do?	Sources
Calcium	Builds and strengthens bones and teeth. Also needed for blood clotting and functioning of nerves and muscles.	Milk, cheese, yogurt, canned fish (when bones included), dark green leafy vegetables, bread, soya beans, nuts and seeds, especially sesame.
Iron	Needed to make red blood cells. Iron deficiency makes children tired and lethargic and may affect development.	Iron from meat, poultry, offal, fish and eggs is the easiest to absorb. Also from green leafy vegetables, cereals, pulses and foods fortified with iron.
Zinc	Essential for wound healing, growth and development.	Found in milk, cheese, meat, eggs, fish, pulses and wholegrain cereals.

Vitamin	What does it do?	Sources
Vitamin A	Needed for growth, healthy skin, vision and development of immune system.	Full-fat milk, cheese, butter, carrots, green leafy vegetables, liver, mangoes, peaches and apricots.
Vitamin D	Helps control calcium absorption and vital for absorption of phosphorus.	Sunlight. Also found in meat, oily fish, eggs and butter. Added to margarine and some cereals.
Vitamin E	Protects cells against damage by free radicals (see glossary on page 85).	Vegetable oils such as soya, corn and olive oil. Also in wholegrain cereals, nuts, seeds and eggs.
Vitamin C	Needed for healthy skin, cartilage, bone and nervous system. Also for iron absorption.	Fruit and vegetables such as apples, berries, citrus fruits, potatoes and green vegetables.
Vitamin K	Essential for clotting of blood and also for normal bone structure.	The body can make vitamin K, but also in green leafy vegetables, cereals and vegetable oils.
B vitamins (B1, B2, B3, B6)	Required to metabolize food and so produce energy, for healthy skin, nervous system and heart.	All the B vitamins except B12 are in bread and whole cereals, nuts and seeds, pulses and green vegetables.
Vitamin B12	For cell division, making red blood cells, a healthy nervous system and to release energy from food.	Meat, salmon, cod, milk, cheese, eggs, yeast extract and seaweed. Vegans need to take it as a supplement.
Folate	For cell division, a healthy nervous system and the formation of blood cells. Helps reduce the risk of neural tube defects in unborn babies.	Found in yeast extract, orange juice, green leafy vegetables and liver. Cereals and bread may be fortified with folic acid (the synthetic form of folate).

Foods from different food groups provide different vitamins and minerals.

Feeding chart

This chart brings together the nutritional information in the book. You can download a printable version by going to **www.usborne-quicklinks.com** and typing in the keywords 'healthy food for babies'.

0 – 6 months

General: Breast or formula milk only.

Foods good for age group: Breast milk or first stage formula milk.

Foods to avoid: Everything else, including other kinds of milk.

Notes: Eat a varied, balanced diet when you are breast-feeding. Don't have more than two portions of oily fish per week, and avoid peanuts if you or a family member has a food allergy, hayfever, asthma or eczema. Limit alcohol and caffeine intake. Try to let your baby feed when they want, for as long as they want.

6 – 8 months

General: Breast or formula milk, and introduce purées and mashed foods.

Foods good for age group: Breast milk or follow-on (second stage) formula milk, baby rice, cream cheese, yogurt, fruit and vegetable purées, mashed food including pulses, fish, lean meat and eggs. Tap water or some types of bottled water, diluted fresh fruit juice – though milk should still be the main drink.

Foods to avoid: Unpasteurized milk or cheese, raw or undercooked eggs, honey, foods with added salt, sugar or artificial sweeteners, bottled waters with a high level of calcium or sodium, tea, coffee, drinks with added sugar, fizzy drinks or fruit-based drinks, whole nuts (because of choking risk). Babies with allergies, hayfever, asthma or eczema in the family should not have peanuts.

Notes: The main aim is to encourage your baby to eat from a spoon. Introduce new foods gradually, first as semi-liquid purées in tiny quantities, later as thicker purées and mashed food. Babies need to learn to chew at 6 to 8 months to help their speech development. From about six months, offer water or milk in a cup between meals – try to wean them off bottles by the time they're one.

9 – 11 months

General: Move from puréed and mashed foods to minced and chopped foods, plus finger foods. Breast or follow-on (second stage) formula milk.

Foods good for age group: As for 6 to 8 months, plus chopped fruit and vegetables, pasta, rice, bread, cheese, yogurt and fromage frais, fresh or canned oily fish, eggs (always well cooked) and some stronger flavours such as herbs, onions, garlic, olives and tiny quantities of milder spices such as black pepper.

Foods to avoid: Whole nuts, and peanuts if there's a family history of allergies. Foods which carry a risk of food poisoning, including: soft, mould-ripened or unpasteurized cheeses, honey, liver pâté and raw or lightly cooked eggs. Foods with added sugar, artificial sweeteners or salt. Babies under a year should have less than 1g salt (0.4g sodium) a day.

Notes: Your baby should now be eating three meals a day with healthy snacks in between. They can start to eat chopped or minced foods and reduce milk intake as they get more energy from food. Encourage them to eat a range of finger foods. If you introduce a wide variety of flavours and textures at this stage, children are less likely to become fussy eaters later on.

1 – 3 years

General: Toddlers can now eat many of the same foods as the rest of the family and can start drinking full-fat cow's milk as their main drink.

Foods good for age group: Most foods apart from the ones listed below.

Foods to avoid: Whole nuts, very hot or spicy foods, raw eggs or eggs with runny yolks, fizzy drinks and squashes, tea, coffee, unpasteurized milk, some fish such as swordfish, shark or marlin, foods with added jam or syrup. Also limit sugar, honey, and salt – no more than 2g of salt (0.8g sodium) in total a day.

Notes: Children under two still have tiny stomachs so need small meals with healthy snacks in between. Their diet should include all the main food groups (see page 10) and a wide variety of foods. They can start drinking full-fat cow's milk as their main drink. Aim to organize mealtimes for about the same time every day, and to keep introducing new foods. Try to make mealtimes happy and sociable occasions.

Weights and measures

All of the recipes in this book provide both metric and imperial measures, but it's useful to know how to convert between the two:

Liquid measures

75ml	2 fl oz	1/8 pint
150ml	5 fl oz	1/4 pint
200ml	7 fl oz	1/3 pint
300ml	10 fl oz	1/2 pint
400ml	14 fl oz	2/3 pint
450ml	15 fl oz	3/4 pint
600ml	20 fl oz	1 pint

Dry measures

30g	1oz	—
55g	2oz	—
85g	3oz	—
125g	4oz	1/4 lb
225g	8oz	1/2 lb
350g	12oz	3/4 lb
450g	16oz	1 lb

For the best results, work with either metric or imperial measures. Don't switch between the two.

Oven temperatures

Oven temperatures can vary considerably from oven to oven, and sometimes the temperature on the dial doesn't precisely match the actual temperature inside the oven, so the times and temperatures listed for the recipes in this book may need adjusting slightly to suit your own oven. Below is a conversion table of oven temperatures which you may also find useful:

160°C	325°F	gas mark 3	Moderate
180°C	350°F	gas mark 4	Moderate
190°C	375°F	gas mark 5	Moderately hot
200°C	400°F	gas mark 6	Moderately hot
220°C	425°F	gas mark 7	Hot
230°C	450°F	gas mark 8	Hot

Fan assisted ovens are usually hotter than other ovens, so check the instruction book to see if you need to lower a temperature. As a rough guide, it's usual to reduce the temperature listed by 25°C (50°F) and the cooking times roughly by 10 minutes for every hour of cooking when using a fan oven.

When you're cooking something in an oven, put it on the middle shelf, unless the recipe says otherwise. When using a grill, position food about 8cm (3in) below the heat source. Any closer risks burning, and any lower means the food takes longer to cook.

Choking

It is very frightening when a child has something stuck in their throat and cannot breathe. If they can't cough the object out, you need to stay calm and act fast.

Babies under one year old

1. Lay the baby face down across your lap, or along your forearm. Make sure their head is lower than their body.

2. Give up to five sharp blows between their shoulder blades with the heel of your hand. Check their mouth after each blow.

3. If the baby is still choking, place two fingers in the middle of their breastbone (one finger's width below the nipple line) and push up to five times.

4. Check their mouth after each thrust. If it is not clear, get medical help.

Babies and toddlers over a year old

1. For toddlers, stand or kneel behind them and wrap both your arms around the top half of their body.

2. Place one of your fists between their belly button and the bottom of their breastbone, between their ribs, and hold on to it with your other hand.

3. Pull the fist upwards and inwards sharply up to five times, but do not use too much force.

4. Check the child's mouth after each thrust. If it is not clear, get medical help.

5. Always take a toddler who has had abdominal thrusts to a doctor to be checked afterwards.

DO NOT USE ABDOMINAL THRUSTS ON BABIES UNDER ONE YEAR OF AGE

Internet links

At the Usborne Quicklinks Website there are links to lots of recommended websites that you may find useful, and other things that you can download. To visit the sites, go to **www.usborne-quicklinks.com** and type in these keywords:

healthy food for babies

Here are some of the things you can do via Usborne Quicklinks:

• Find more advice about breast-feeding and bottle-feeding.

• Download the feeding chart from pages 88—89 of this book.

• Find more recipes suitable for babies and toddlers at different stages.

• Discover more information about children with food allergies.

Internet safety

The websites recommended in Usborne Quicklinks are regularly reviewed. However, the content of a website may change at any time and Usborne Publishing is not responsible for the content or availability of websites other than its own.

General index

Recipe index

With thanks to...

Staff, parents and children at Cannons Health Club Nursery, Surbiton;
Eleanor Salanson; Matej Geralsky; Gulia, Nicholas and Chiara Held;
Molly McNicholas; Steadyco® for using their 'Let's EAT' range of
tableware for children (p53); The Cotswold Company;
Emma Helbrough, Sam Taplin, Jessica Greenwell and Claire Masset
for editorial assistance, indexing, picture and website research.

Photo credits:

The publishers are grateful to the following for permission to reproduce material:
p24 © Gallo Images/Alamy; p33 © James Woodson/Digital Vision/Getty Images

Additional illustrations: Dubravka Kolanovic

Digital imaging: Keith Furnival

The websites described in this book are regularly reviewed and updated on Usborne Quicklinks, however the content of a website
may change at any time and Usborne Publishing is not responsible, and does not accept liability, for the content or availability of
any website other than its own, or for any exposure to harmful, offensive or inaccurate material which may appear on the Web.
For more information, see the 'Net Help' area of the Usborne Quicklinks Website at www.usborne-quicklinks.com